TABLE OF CONTENTS

INTRODUCTION

You are a woman, and you do not have much money. You cannot save money. The advice offered in magazines and newspapers does not help you because you don't have enough money to begin to do what they recommend. You do not have money to "invest" in stocks and bonds and mutual funds. You worry about how to pay for your children's education. Or you worry about having enough for retirement, or to buy a home. In fact, you often seem to have barely enough money to make ends meet.

You have no education about handling your money except that you've been told all your life to "shop wisely." So you clip coupons. You go from store to store buying the foods and clothing that are on "sale." You stand in the supermarkets and compare prices. Usually, you buy the cheapest products on the shelves. You buy higher fat hamburger instead of ground round steak. You buy the store brands of detergent and canned goods. You try to buy in large, family size quantitites. Still, no matter how wisely you shop, you remain poor, or at least not rich. And you still cannot save any money.

The first lesson you should learn is that if you depend on "shopping" to save money, you will always be poor. There are many good reasons for this. First, women are taught to shop 'til they drop because buying keeps the American economy rolling right along. When you watch the evening news on TV, have you ever noticed that it's good news for the American economy when consumers go on a buying spree? The more they spend at Christmas, the more new cars they buy, the more new homes they buy, the better off the economy is. What these same newscasts rarely report is that these buying sprees that keep the American economy chugging along keep individual households in debt. It seems a very peculiar thing that when the broader American economy is going very well, that individual households can be setting themselves up for personal disaster through too much debt, but that's the way it is.

Secondly, when you shop, you are actually the victim or pawn of sophisticated marketing techniques that influence what you buy and how much you will spend for each product. Americans spend more than four trillion dollars on consumer goods and services each year. I worked for 25 years in the market research profession. My job was to try to understand consumers so that my clients--usually large corporations--could persuade you to buy their products. Marketing research professionals follow you with hidden cameras. Marketers, trying to get you to buy more and more goods and services that you don't really need, hire anthropologists, and psychologists to observe you and your daily behavior. They design their packaging and their advertising to create *wants* in you for things that are not necessary to your well being, but you think they are.

The third reason you won't get rich from shopping is that the best way to get rich is to hang onto your money. When you shop, you spend money, and as I will explain later on, you are spending very expensive money. You are spending **after tax dollars** on consumer goods rather than on **capital goods.**

Therefore, the fact remains that when you spend your money on most consumer goods and services, you make the U.S. economy fat, and you keep yourself poor. Shopping in general and comparison shopping specifically, except for very large items such as cars or appliances, are a waste of your time and your money. You don't know that, and most women's magazines will not tell you that because their advertisers want you to keep right on shopping and shopping.

This book will introduce some new concepts of money handling that go beyond mere shopping. It will give you new ways of thinking about your time and your money. This book is not about investing in the stock market. It will tell you little about buying insurance. This book is for those women who do not yet have enough money to even think about investing in the stock market or buying more insurance. The purpose of this book is to help you save that first $1,000 - $5,000, and *then you can begin investing in the stock market.* This book will help you think about money the way businessmen think of money--as a commodity to be used to make more money, as a tool to buy the things you want in life, as a means of expanding the scope and enjoyment of your life.

You may have been told all your life that "Money is the root of all evil." Money is not the root of all evil. Money is a tool, like a hammer or a potato peeler. How you handle your money can lead to evil; money in and of itself cannot. Greed certainly leads to evil, but so does poverty. Desiring money to further your education or that of your children, to expand your sense of well being, your happiness, and to prepare for a secure and comfortable old age is a worthy goal, but this will not simply happen. You've got to make it happen.

You may believe that women should leave all the money handling to their husbands or the men in their lives because men are "smarter" about money. No data support the idea that men are more intelligent about handling money than women are. In fact, some data suggest the opposite: that women are more cautious, more thoughtful about money handling while men tend to splurge on big items, to take greater financial risks. The differences in money handling between men and women result from differences in experience and education, not any innate intelligence or sex determined brain power.

When you begin to take an active interest in your family's finances, you may find yourself fighting against your husband and his ideas of power and money handling. You must risk this for your own future financial safety. Too many women become victims of their financial ignorance. Your husband may die suddenly, and you will find yourself faced with handling all the finances. Or your husband or lover may leave you. Or you may discover that your husband has been cheating on your income taxes and you are now liable for all the payments. Or you may discover that your husband or lover has made some very risky investments in the stock market that could leave you bankrupt, impoverished in your old age. For all these reasons, you **must** learn how to handle money effectively.

You may think you don't have the time to learn how to handle money. Of all the ways you can spend your time, handling money is one of the best. When you handle your money effectively, your entire life moves along better. You achieve greater security and comfort.

You may shrug off the importance of money in your life, saying that you can get along without giving it much thought, that you don't need much money to be happy. That may be true now, while you are young and healthy, but it will not be true when you are eighty years old and either widowed or divorced or unmarried.

Men spend their lives pursuing money while women are taught not to think about money. Women learn that thinking about money is "unfeminine." A woman who believes that knowing about money is unfeminine chooses to be a victim, at the mercy of the men in her life--either husband, family members, lawyers, accountants, physicians, and other male professionals who enter her life during accidents, catastrophes, or simply bad luck. Having money and knowing about money is not bad. Knowledge of money gives women power. When a woman controls her money, she controls her life.

Being poor is not feminine either. The most important thing for you to remember is that in the United States, the majority of poor people are either single women or female heads of households with children. Women accounted for nearly three quarters of the elderly poor in 1990. The average income for women over age 65 is $6,300 per year. Women live an average of seven years longer than men and therefore often run out of retirement money. If you depend only on social security for your retirement income, you will be poor. The average *monthly* social security benefit paid out in 1993 was only $653. A widow or widower received even less on average: only $608 per month.

On average, women who divorce experience a 73% drop in their standard of living based on their household income. That means, if your family earned $100,000 per year when you were married, after your divorce, you may only receive about $25,000 per year.

Being poor is hard work. It saps your energy. You work twice as hard as wealthier people, yet you receive less for your efforts. Lack of money leads to wasting your precious time. If you can't afford a car, you must ride on public transit systems. More often than not, this means waiting at the bus stop, in rain, heat, snow, for buses that run late. When you arrive at your job late, this creates a bad impression on your boss, and will lead to fewer or lower pay raises, or even firing from your job.

Being poor means you waste money. Because you have no savings, you delay necessary maintenance on your car, your home, your applicances. Then they break down and your repair bills are much larger. You delay going to the doctor until you are really sick, and the bills are therefore higher. Without savings, you buy things on installment credit, which means you may pay twice as much for your clothing and appliances as you would if you could pay for them with cash.

You do not have to live this way. You can choose to change. You can learn to control your money and thus control your life.

If you have read this far, you know that you want to gain this control. You will need these tools to manage your money and your life:

Self discipline

Hard work

A calculator. You can buy a good solar powered calculator for about $10. Pick one that has big comfortable buttons for you to push and a clear display screen. You only need a calculator that adds, subtracts, multiplies and divides. More complicated functions are not necessary. Do not worry if you have been poor at arithmetic. The calculations in this book are simple, but essential.

Throughout this book, when I introduce a concept that will help you think about money differently, I will **bold face** it to call attention to it so that you can learn what it means.

Now, let's get started.

SECTION ONE: SPENDING YOUR TIME EFFECTIVELY

CHAPTER ONE: TIME VERSUS MONEY

If there is one concept I want you to learn and to learn in your very bones, it is the concept of **time versus money**. You have two assets to help you earn money: your time and your money. The two are interchangeable. In these first chapters, I will concentrate on teaching you how to use your time to earn money more effectively.

Your time is valuable. It is valuable because it is limited. You may only have about 70 years of productive time to use in your life.

Women tend not to value their time. This is no accident. Men often do not value women's time either. If there is no dollar value placed on women's work, society treats women's work as useless or without value. This is shown by the fact that a woman who does not work for wages does not get social security benefits. She gets the benefits earned by her husband, despite the fact that she may have spent thirty years cooking, cleaning, rearing children. It also shows in the fact that even when they work in comparable jobs, men earn more money than women. When women start valuing their time, stop wasting it on silliness, then men will begin to value women's work.

When you calculate **time versus money,** you decide whether you have more time to do something yourself, or more money to pay someone else to do it for you. For every task you undertake, either at your home, at your volunteer activities, or at your job, you need to know whether it makes more sense for you to pay for that task with money you have earned at your job, or to pay for it with your time. If you are not working for wages outside the home, you still need to calculate whether it makes more financial sense for you to do a task yourself or to hire someone else to do it.

Time versus money is the basic economic calculation used in all business. Your doctor charges you by the hour. Your lawyer charges by the hour. Your auto mechanic charges by the hour. Your own employer probably pays you by the hour. Certainly, whether you receive a salary or not, your employer thinks of your value to the company in hourly rates.

Women spend their time on tasks that are essentially useless work. This is another reason why women's time is not valued by men and by society. Women scrub kitchen floors daily, not for cleanliness but to make them *shine*. They scrub and wash and fluff to get clothes *white* instead of merely clean. They worry about ring around the collar. This is silliness. Men know it's silliness. Women must still learn this. One reason men won't help with the housework is because most of it is silliness, and they have other things to do with their time.

Women donate their time without considering its value. They treat their time as though it were "free." So they make coffee and cookies for their churches. They make little embroidered dodads for Christmas bazaars, for their children's schools or their churches. They collect money for the various charities, going door to door in their neighborhoods. Women don't receive money for these volunteer activities, but they are work. They are unpaid work, and they destroy your time. Why won't men give their time to many of these kinds of activities? Because they know they earn nothing for the time expended, except maybe a little pat on the back--not very solid retirement income.

Women do not insist on getting top dollar for the paid work they actually do. They think that the men who are their bosses will pay them "what they are worth," and they trust in equity and fairness. I recently heard of a young woman who is not wealthy, a single mother with no health insurance, no steady means of support. She accepted a job finishing some hardwood floors in a mountain cabin near where I live. The builder offered to pay her $20 an hour but she said, "Oh no, that's too much!" She devalues herself and all women with that answer. She thinks she's being noble, or fair, or generous, but she is simply being stupid. With an attitude like that, people will always take advantage of her. The goal of *working* should be to earn as much money for every minute spent in work as is humanly possible without being viciously greedy.

What is work? Except when you sleep or play or eat, every minute you spend of every day on any activity can be defined as work. You either work within your home or you work outside of your home earning wages paid by an employer, or you work as some sort of unpaid volunteer. Most women do all of these types of work. Work includes transportation time: the time you spend either in your car or on public transit or walking to either your job, to stores, to the bank, or even to your church. You either need to get paid for transportation time, or you need to keep the time spent traveling to a bare minimum.

Now that you can see most of your life is taken up with work, the next step in your money management plan is to determine how many dollars per hour your time is worth. How much are you actually earning per hour of work? In other words, you must determine your **time versus money** value.

There are two ways of doing this. If you are employed, you can use the wages you are paid at your job as your value per hour. Use your wages **pretax** as the basis for your calculations. That is, if your wages **before taxes and withholding** are $250 per week for a 38 hour week, your hourly rate is:

<ins>CALCULATION:</ins> $250 divided by 38 = $6.57 per hour.

This is what your time is worth in the labor market. If you work at a job that pays you $25,000 a year for 40 hour weeks, your hourly rate is:

<ins>CALCULATION:</ins> $25,000 divided by 2080 hours in a year (40 x 52 weeks), which equals $12.02 an hour, **pretax**.

You should calculate all of your at-home activities, your volunteer activities, and your travel time, at the hourly rate you receive at your job. If you work at a job that pays you $15,000 a year for 40 hour weeks, your hourly rate is about $7.21 an hour, and you should calculate all of your at home activities at that rate.

> CALCULATION: $15,000 divided by 2080 hours per year = $7.21 per hour.

For the purposes of this book, if you are a full time housewife and *do not work outside the home for wages,* I am going to value your time as worth $10 an hour. If you have worked outside the home, use the wages you would be earning if you were still at that job.

Use these wage rates to calculate the value of your labor at home versus the prices you have to pay for services and products. Now, how can you apply this information to your financial decision making?

Example: Charitable donations: I was asked to bake a pie for a bake sale for a local charity. I purchased the fruit for the pie, spent about an hour preparing the pie, used my stove to bake it, and then drove it to the charity sale. They sold the pie for $2.50. How much did that pie actually "cost"? Let's make a rough estimate:

Ingredients:	$1.00
My time to bake it at $10 an hour:	$5.00
Electricity to heat the stove to bake the pie:	.50
Gas to drive the pie to the charity:	.50
Total cost of the pie:	$7.00

I would have been better off and so would the charity if I had simply given them $7.00. I could have taken it off my income tax as a deduction, which in the 31% tax bracket means I would have actually only donated about $5.00. The charity would have had real money of $7.00 instead of only $2.50. Furthermore, I could have used the hour I spent baking the pie on other activities that would have either been more pleasurable or more economically productive.

Another example: You look at the price of a product that you buy ready-made in the stores, and then you calculate how much it would cost you to make the same product for yourself at home. This is also true for services. For example, if you have a leaking faucet in your bathroom, you can either:

1. Fix it yourself
2. Call a plumber

To fix it yourself, you may have to buy a wrench, or a pair of pliers and a screwdriver, the washer, and perhaps a how-to book on plumbing. Let's say the total cost comes to about $15 to fix your own dripping faucet. A plumber may charge you anywhere between $30 and $60 to come to your home to make this repair. Obviously, it is cheaper to pay $15 to repair the faucet yourself than to pay a plumber.

At this stage of your life, it is probably almost always going to be more economical for you to "do-it-yourself" than to pay someone else to do it for you.

Here is another example of a **time versus money** calculation: I watched a television program a few years ago about a woman who was a champion coupon clipper. A four drawer filing cabinet full of coupons for purchases at the super market occupied one wall of her dining room. Every day, she scanned the newspapers and various magazines for coupons. She estimated that she "saved" $2,000 a year clipping coupons. She estimated how many hours she spent looking for and clipping coupons. When I divided the amount of money she "saved" ($2,000 per year) by the number of hours she spent clipping coupons (about 1,330), her actual "earnings" were only *$1.50 per hour.* She might have spent her time more wisely working at a fast food restaurant or some other job that paid $5 an hour or more. This is a **time versus money** calculation.

Obviously, other factors enter into this calculation. If the woman has to hire a baby-sitter, has to drive 5 miles to a fast food restaurant, and has to pay income taxes on her wages, she probably does save more money clipping coupons than going out of the house to work. I will discuss these so-called **hidden costs or costs of doing business** later in this book. But the important thing here is to calculate out how much time you are spending on a given task, and does it make economic sense to do it. Remember, you will calculate out your **time versus your money** by:

1) Using your hourly wage at work as a guide, and then calculating whether you can make or do the thing or service cheaper yourself compared with hiring some else to do it for you.

2) Or you will assign a value to your work based on what you could earn if you got a job outside the home, or you can use $10 per hour, which is a low but basically a living wage of $20,800 per year for forty hour weeks.

There is another method of calculating **time versus money**. You estimate how much money and time you spend doing some task at home, and then you multiply the rate per minute out so that you get an hourly rate. (Note: I will mention **after tax, non taxable,** and **pretax** dollars below. I will discuss these terms in greater detail later in this book, but I'd like you to begin thinking in these terms.)

Let's use so-called convenience foods as an example of a time versus money equation. For example, prepared salad dressings in a supermarket vary in price, but I recently priced two: one at $5.16 a quart and one at $4.76 a quart. If you earn $10 an hour at your job, you must work about 30 minutes to pay for a quart of those salad dressings. On the other hand, a quart of salad dressing can be made at home in about 5 minutes. So let's cost out the amount of money you could earn per hour by making your own salad dressings at home.

<ins>CALCULATION:</ins> List of ingredients for one quart of salad dressing.

1. A quart of mayonnaise costs $2.39
2. A quart of salad oil costs about $2.52
3. The seasonings cost pennies.
4. Time to mix up a quart -- about 5 minutes.
5. Total cost to make a quart of home made salad dressing -- about $2.70

If it costs you about $5 to buy a quart of prepared salad dressing at the market and $2.70 to make it at home, subtract the difference: result -- you have saved $2.30 for 5 minutes of your work. Multiply this $2.30 times 12 (the number of 5 minute units in an hour) and you find you have earned **tax free or non taxable** money at the rate of $27.60 per hour.

I priced thousand island salad dressing recently. My mother taught me to make it when I was thirteen years old. A quart of thousand island salad dressing costs about $6.11 in the store. To make thousand island, you take some mayonnaise, ketchup, some Parmesan cheese, a little milk, some Tabasco if you like, maybe add some sweet pickle relish, and mix it all together until you get a texture and a taste that you like. You could make a quart of thousand island for about $2.60 compared with paying $6.11 a quart for ready made--a savings of $3.51 for 5 minutes of work at home. If it takes you five minutes to make a quart of salad dressing, multiply $3.51 x 12 (the number of 5 minute units in an hour) = $42.12 an hour of **tax free earnings** for your time.

I *never* buy prepared salad dressings. They are too easy and too cheap to make at home. When I visit my friends' homes, and the hostess sets out three or four of these fancy shaped bottles of salad dressing on the table, I know money is being wasted, and this woman has yet to learn the value of her **time versus her money.**

Let's do this exercise again. Potatoes cost about $1.89 per five pounds. Five pounds of potatoes equals 80 ounces (5 lbs x 16 oz = 80 oz). Let's assume that one serving of potatoes equals four ounces. Thus, you can get twenty servings of potatoes out of a 5 pound bag (80 ounces divided by 4 = 20 servings). The per serving cost of cooking your own potatoes is about 10 cents: $1.89 divided by 20 servings = 9.45 cents.

Now, compare this with buying instant mashed potatoes in the store. The cost of the package is $2.46 per pound and the package says it will provide ten servings of potatoes.

<u>CALCULATION:</u> $2.46 divided by 10 servings = 25 cents per serving versus about 10 cents per serving when you cook potatoes out of the bag.

You can save 15 cents per serving by cooking and mashing your own potatoes. If you add 5 minutes of your time to peel and mash the potatoes, you have actually earned money at the rate of:

<u>CALCULATION:</u> 60 minutes divided by 5 minutes (the time you took to peel potatoes) = 12 units.
12 x 15 cents per serving = $1.80 per serving
$1.80 x 5 servings = $9.00 per hour wages you have earned, **after tax** by preparing five servings of your own potatoes instead of buying instant mashed.

Notice how much more money you can earn per hour by making your own salad dressings. If you make a **time versus money** calculation, you can see that if your time is really short, it makes sense for you to learn to make your own salad dressings rather than mash your own potatoes, but both are worth doing at home rather than buying prepackaged foods.

I recently priced some TV dinners. On sale, one 7.5 ounce serving of chicken breast and potatoes cost $2.00. This comes out to $4.26 per pound for potatoes and chicken.

<u>CALCULATION</u>: 16 ounces (one pound) divided by 7.5 oz = 2.13 x $2.00 = $4.26 per pound cost of the TV dinner.

Recently you could buy one pound of chicken breasts for about $1.89 and 5 pounds of potatoes for about $2.50, enough for three or four meals of chicken and potatoes for a total of $4.39, or about $1.00 per meal versus $2.00 per meal. If you serve four TV dinners, the cost will be $8.00 instead of $4.00 if you were to make the meals from scratch. In addition, you still have a lot of potatoes in the bag after you've cooked your dinners If you spend 30 minutes cooking this dinner for 4 people, you earn at a rate of $8.00 per hour **after tax**.

CALCULATION: **4 meals x $1.00 each (the money you have saved by doing it yourself) = $4.00 x 2(there are two thirty minute periods per hour) = $8.00 per hour earned after tax.**

No matter that the "price" of buying the TV dinners seems so cheap at $2.00 per package. They are very expensive compared to buying the raw materials and cooking the dinner yourself. When you buy TV dinners, you pay for the ingredients (chicken and potatoes), the labor to put them in the package already cooked, the packaging, the marketing and advertising to encourage you to buy them, and the costs of the store which sells the product. Why should you pay for all this stuff that you don't need? You need chicken and potatoes, not any of that other stuff.

All right, you say, this is nonsense. What's a few pennies here and there for mashed potatoes and salad dressing? TV dinners save me time.

First, you don't have a lot of money or you wouldn't be reading this book.

Second, the only way you can accumulate money, that first $1,000 of **capital**, is in small increments in every area of your life. You don't have $1,000 or big bucks to save in one fell swoop. Your only alternative is what I call "The Great Barrier Reef" theory of home economics. Little deposits made every day create a big structure at the end of a year or two.

Third, TV dinners don't really save you time. They simply redistribute how you spend your time. Remember, you have a finite life span. You can either choose to spend your time on **short term** activities or products, or you can spend your time on **long term** activities or products. You can spend your time to pay for convenience or you can spend your time to pay for **capital accumulation.** Convenience wastes your money. **Capital accumulation** increases your money.

Spending money on unnecessary convenience such as TV dinners means you either have to work longer hours at your job to pay for that convenience, or you have to do without other things in your life. If you work at a $5.00 an hour job, you will have to work about a half hour to pay for one TV dinner. If you were to make that dinner from scratch, you have to work only about 15 minutes to pay for it.

Yes, you transfer that 15 minutes from your job to your home, where you must prepare the dinner yourself, but at home you are earning money at a rate of about $8.00 an hour **after tax**. Does it make more sense to work longer hours at your job, where you earn only $5.00 an hour **pretax** rather than working more hours at home where you earn at a rate of between $8.00 and $40.00 per hour, **after tax,** depending on what you are doing with your time?

If there is anything that totally depresses me, it is to see a woman who works eight hour days at a job which pays her only $7.00 an hour **pretax**, and on the way home from work, this same woman blows all that hard earned money away by buying TV dinners and other prepared foods at the market, instead of making them herself. She is not only spinning her wheels, she's going backwards financially.

Let's look at another very important way that cooking at home can save/earn significant amounts of money for yourself and your family. You eat at home instead of in restaurants or cafeterias.

For years, I was the only person in the lunch room of my corporation who ate out of a brown bag. I received a lot of teasing about this, about being so "cheap." When I returned from my third trip to Europe though, my fellow employees expressed their envy of old "money bags" who can go to Europe whenever she wants. I pointed out to them that bringing my own lunch to work for five days a week, fifty weeks a year, paid for my trips to Europe. Here's the arithmetic:

<u>CALCULATION:</u>

Cost of leftovers for brown bag lunches (pieces of broiled chicken, yogurt, salads, tuna salads, fruit, cookies)	$1.50
Times 5 days a week	7.50

Times 50 working weeks in a year $375.00

<u>Compared with restaurant or cafeteria lunches:</u>

Assume $5.00 for each meal eaten out x 5 days
a week: $25.00

Times fifty weeks $1,250.00
for lunches purchased at restaurants or cafeterias.

I saved approximately $875 in one year by making my own lunches at home and taking them to work. Air fare to Europe has been running around $600 recently. I've been very conservative at pricing lunches in restaurants for the above calculations. You can readily pay $10 or more per lunch in some cities.

If it takes you ten minutes a day, five days a week to make your own brown bag lunch, it will take you a total of 2500 minutes a year (50 minutes per week x 50 weeks) or 41.66 hours per year to make lunches.

Divide $875 (the amount saved by not buying at a restaurant) by 41.66 hours and you find you have earned money at the rate of $21.00 an hour **after tax wages** by making your own lunches at home. Doesn't it seem stupid to you to earn less than $10 an hour **pretax** at your job and then waste that money buying lunches instead of making them for yourself?

In addition to cooking, do-it-yourself home repairs are another excellent way of earning **after tax** dollars home. It is true, you will have to teach yourself how to make these repairs, and you will also need to teach yourself how to cook, but the investment of time will save you big bucks during the course of your life. You can buy how-to books at the local hardware stores and lumberyards, or you can check them out of the library.

House repairs can be very hard work for a woman. You may find that you do not have the physical strength to do some of them. You may have to call a professional for help, but remember if you invest the time in learning how to repair a leaking faucet, you will have that skill at your beck and call forever. After your initial investment in learning how to repair a faucet, each time you repair a faucet, the cost becomes cheaper and cheaper. This concept is called **amortization.**

That is, the initial cost of your tools and the investment in your education (buying a wrench, screw drivers, a pair of pliers and a book on how to do small plumbing repairs) is spread across all the repairs you make in the future. Each time you make a repair using your tools and your knowledge, the cost of that repair decreases.

The first time you repair a faucet, it may cost you $15 because you have had to buy the book and the tools. The next time you repair a faucet, the cost will be half -- $7.50-- because you don't have to replace your knowledge or your tools. You've already bought them. The third time you repair a faucet, the cost will be about $5.00, and so on. You can begin to see how tools *earn money for you.* The more frequently you use them, the more money you earn from them. This is why tools are a **capital investment.** Over time, tools earn money for you rather than stealing it from you. The term **capital investment** will be used and discussed again later, but for now, just remember that tools earn money for you, and education is one of the best tools you have to earn money for yourself.

Notice that if you call a plumber each time you need a faucet repaired, your costs will *increase* each time instead of decrease. The plumber will keep raising his rates to keep up with his own costs and inflation.

If you earn *less* at your job than you would pay someone else to do the work for you, it makes sense for you to do-it-yourself. If you earn $7.50 per hour at your job, and you must pay a house painter $30 an hour to paint your house or apartment, it makes big dollars and cents for you to paint your own home during your off hours of work.

Over time, you will learn which jobs you can handle and which you must hire someone else to do for you. I always paint my own house. I spackle too. I stain woodwork. I change my faucet washers, and repair small leaks in my shower heads. I do very minor electrical repairs. I build everything I can that does not demand really fine carpentry work. This past fall, I built a huge workbench in my garage, a doghouse, a 6 foot by 3 foot by 2 foot deep planter box. I built two sets of shelves for the garage and hung other shelves and boards from which to hang my shovels, rakes, etc.

I do minor maintenance on my snowmobile. I used to change the oil on my lawn tractor. Where I live now, in the mountains, I have learned how to sharpen my chain saw and to dismantle and clean it periodically.

Some people swear that hanging wallpaper is easy, but I have never tackled that job.

Investing the time and energy to read the instruction manuals that come with your purchases, to learn how to take things apart and put them back together again, is tedious, but it saves you money in the long run. Buying home repair tools is expensive at first, but you need only buy them once, keep them in good order, and they will last a lifetime.

If you cannot understand the directions, or you cannot figure out how to do something, get someone to show you how. I've had to ask the men up here on this mountain to show me how to fill my snowmobile battery, clean the spark plugs, adjust my chain saw, and do many other tasks that I could not figure out myself. They laugh and tease me about my ignorance, but I do not mind. A person must do what has to be done to get the job done, and I know a lot of things, sewing for example, that they know nothing about. It cuts both ways.

Sewing is another important home activity that can save you a lot of money. Frankly, I hate sewing, but this is one of the most effective ways to earn money at home. This is especially true if you sew your own party clothes.

When I finally began to earn good money at my job, I stopped sewing my woolen work suits, and bought them. I bought my winter coats too, but I always sew party clothes, because they are usually very expensive to buy, and you only wear them once or twice.

A few years ago, I decided I wanted a Christmas suit. At that time in the local department store, I found that tapestry two piece suits were selling for about $500 each. The prices knocked me out of my socks. So, when in New York on business one day, I stopped in the fabric district on the West Side and bought tapestry fabric and silk for a blouse, lining fabric, thread, and notions for a total of $125. It took me no more than ten hours to sew the suit--completely lined and inner lined, hand stitched hems. My Christmas suit cost me in time and money about $250.00 (figuring my time at $10 an hour). By saving that $250 off the price of a store bought suit, I actually earned money at home at the rate of $25 an hour, **after tax** ($250 divided by 10 hours - $25.00 per hour).

If I work at a job that pays me $10 an hour, I must work 60 hours, more than a full week, to pay for a Christmas suit that costs $500.00. First, I'll have to work about 15 hours at $10 to pay the taxes (estimated at 30% for federal, state, and social security). That comes to $150. Then I'll have to work 50 more hours to pay the $500 for the suit itself. In fact, I have to earn a total of $650 **pretax** to pay for the Christmas suit in the store.

When I lived near Princeton, NJ, I took three tailoring classes and two basic sewing classes at my local adult schools in Princeton and Hopewell Townships. When I sew my own clothing, it usually looks pretty good. I can sew rapidly. Taking sewing courses or taking cooking courses is a **capital investment** in your education that I highly recommend.

Even if you don't want to sew your own clothing, there are many kinds of rough sewing that can save you good money. I had a young woman working for me who put her three children into a day care center near our offices. This day care center required that all the children have "sleeping sacks" for their naps. This young woman could not find any sleeping sacks for less than about $20 each, which meant that she would spend a total of $60 for sleeping sacks for her three children. I suggested that she go to a discount store and buy one big polyester comforter, cut it up into pieces, and sew three sleeping sacks out of it. She followed my advice. She borrowed her mother's sewing machine and did just that, using a comforter that cost her $20. She saved herself $40, money that she did not have, by sewing.

At the time, she worked for me earning $5 an hour, **pretax**. After deducting her income taxes and social security taxes, her **after tax** income was about $3.50 an hour. At that rate, she would have had to work about 17 hours to pay for three sleeping sacks:

<u>CALCULATION:</u> $60 divided by $3.50 = 17 hours.

She only worked about two hours to sew them at home. Thus, to save $40 by sewing her own sleep sacks, she earned money at home at the rate of $20 an hour, **after tax.**

It takes time to learn how to sew, to learn "pattern language." As much as I have sewn, I often find the pattern instructions confusing and incomplete. In fact, I find the instructions for *everything* to be confusing nowadays. Nonetheless, you must simply decide to sit down, glue your rear end to a chair and educate yourself. You will make mistakes, but over the **long term** your investment in education and tools will pay you back many times.

Personal care is another area where spending your time instead of your money will pay off. I realize that most women won't take this gamble, but I'm going to suggest it any way: cut your own hair.

How much do you spend every six weeks at the hair care salon? The last time I had my hair professionally cut was about twenty years ago, and at that time it cost me $25.00. A friend of mine recently told me she spends $60 on a cut and a permanent.

If you spend $60 every six weeks on hair care, you are spending $520 a year. Think about cutting or trimming your own hair. I've been doing it for years now. Granted, my hair doesn't always look perfect, but my friends still go out into public places with me, so it can't look all that bad. Practice helps.

If you earn $10 an hour at your job, it will take you about 52 hours on the job to pay for your hair cuts and perms for a year: over one week's labor out of your precious life to pay for HAIR CARE! We are not talking about using your time for truly valuable experiences and services like education, health care, and vacations.

If you do not want to chance cutting your own hair, cut your children's hair or your husband's. Yesterday, I found my neighbor cutting her husband's hair on a sunny morning, out on their deck. He says it saves him $7.00 each time she does it. She has bought an inexpensive set of battery operated hair clippers at Wal-Mart, and she has gotten better with practice. I used to cut my husband's hair, which took me about ten minutes every couple of weeks, and saved us both precious time and money that we spent elsewhere.

I am not even going to discuss NAIL CARE! When my niece told me how much she spends on nail care to get those long, useless fingernails, I nearly collapsed. A friend just told me she spends $25 a month maintaining her nails. If you spend this kind of money on personal care, you deserve to stay poor.

In addition to **time versus money,** when you think of how to use your time, think of the **long term versus the short term**. This raises the whole issue of your personal values. You've got to decide what is really important to you; what makes you really happy for longer periods of time rather than merely satisfied for a few minutes.

Restaurant meals are fun, but they have only **short term value.** You eat them, have fun, and walk out the door to forget them. A trip to Europe can have **long term value.** You will remember it for years after it is over. You will have learned things and seen things that will occupy your mind and enrich your life until you die. You will see some movies with greater enjoyment because "you've been there." You will read some books with greater insight, because "you've been there."

I once read that the middle class differed from the very rich and the very poor in one way: the middle class *deferred gratification* They controlled their appetites until they had enough money to pay for them. They postponed immediate gratification in favor of long term rewards. Poor people don't have enough money to defer gratification. They can't wait for the next sale; they don't have enough money saved to tide them over. Rich people don't have to defer gratification. They have so much money, they can spend it whenever they want. Actually, this is a myth, but it makes a point.

Convenience is another word for instant gratification. Convenience, instant gratification, cost you money, lots of money. It may be inconvenient to make your own lunches, to sew your own clothes, to fix your own faucets, but over the long run, you will earn big dollars by tolerating this "inconvenience." The difference between an adult human being and a child, is that the child has to have it "now". An adult knows that waiting is usually the best way to get what he wants.

You save money by controlling your spending. You delay immediate spending and wait for a more opportune moment, or you decide not to spend at all.

The second way you save money is to budget your time. I always see advice on financial budgeting in the women's magazines and newspapers, but I see very little about budgeting one's time, and if you are poor, I believe budgeting your time is more important than budgeting your money.

I will talk about financial budgets later in this book, but for now, think about how you spend your time. If possible, keep a notebook of how you spend the hours in your day. You will find where your time goes--whether it goes to earn more money, whether it goes to give you genuine happiness and pleasure, or whether you simply fritter it away on nonsense.

Do you watch the local news on TV? If so, why? You only learn about a bunch of local disasters--murders, fires, rapes, thefts. You need to know this? Hardly! You need to know how to make salad dressing.

If push comes to shove, turn the TV up loud, and *listen* to it while you cook. Better yet, turn it off.

Learn to say "no." I think "no" must be the hardest word to learn for a woman. There is a wonderful country western tune with words to the effect of, "What part of "no" don't you understand?"

You must say "no" to your friends who call you late at night and rouse you from your needed sleep. Stop answering your phone after 9 p.m. I had a colleague who had a friend who insisted on calling her at 11 p.m. or midnight. My friend showed up at work with bags under her eyes all the time. My feeling is that people who do that to you are not your friends. They are merely takers.

Say "no" to your mother, your mother-in-law, your husband, your children. "No" to your church. "No" to your own sense of what ought to be done. I have a friend who washes and waxes her kitchen floor every day. I think she is out of her mind. What a way to spend your life! When you are dying and your life passes through your memory, are you really going to derive comfort from the fact that you washed and waxed your kitchen floor every day?

Do you carefully fold all the clean laundry before putting it into drawers? Why? What difference does it make if your underwear is wrinkled. Get your kids and husband to fold their own laundry. Do you spend extra time trying to keep your whites white in the laundry? Then stop buying whites, or stop worrying when white turns gray. My socks are far from white anymore, but who in the hell is looking at my socks? If they are, I want out of there. That kind of person is not someone I wish to spend my valuable life with.

If you are spending hours commuting to a job, think about changing jobs or moving to a different housing location.

Cut out idle chatter with your neighbors. Don't stay for the coffee hour after church. I used to do that, and when I got home, I wondered why. I hadn't learned anything. I hadn't even really shared anything. I'd just spent some time in useless pleasantries with people I didn't much care for.

Stop reading the newspapers, or only read them once or twice a week. The amount of time people waste reading newspapers is appalling. It's like watching TV news. What in the name of heaven do you learn from reading most sections of the newspapers? How does it make you happier? What have you learned that will stay with you longer than five minutes?

You need your time. You need it to get proper sleep and rest. You can't make money when you are tired. You can't be a good wife, a good mother, a good employee, a good anything if you are exhausted. When I had a phone, I put it on my answering machine for long hours of the day, and refused to answer it except at my convenience. If anyone called me after 9 p.m., I made damned sure they didn't make that mistake again. Here on this mountain, I have put the word out--I write until 2 p.m. Please don't stop by for a social call before then.

When you value your time, other people will value their time with you. If you treat your time as of no account, other people will sop it up, drain you dry for their own sakes. Budget your time. Make notes of what time makes you happiest, makes the people in your life the happiest. Then weed out all the wasted uses of your time. The best way to determine what is a good use of your time and a bad use is to try to remember what you did yesterday. If you cannot remember a single thing you did that gave you pleasure or enhanced your family's life, or earned you some money, then you've wasted that day.

CHAPTER TWO: WHEN IS A DOLLAR NOT A DOLLAR?

In the preceding chapter, I referred to **pretax, tax free or non taxable,** and **after tax** dollars. In this chapter, I will explain the meaning of those terms in greater detail.

You probably think that one dollar always equals one dollar; that a dollar always holds 100 cents. In the world of money management, this is not true. In the world of money management, there are at least four different kinds of dollars, and each has a different value for you, the individual person. To make money in the American economy, you need to begin to think of ways of allocating your work and your money into categories that provide the *richest* possible dollars.

Starting with the worst first, the poorest kind of dollar is a **pretax** dollar. This dollar is like a balloon: it looks big and well rounded, but it's really full of hot air. That's because this dollar exists before any federal or state income taxes have been taken out of it, but by now you know that most dollars have taxes taken out of them sooner or later. Another word for a **pretax** dollar is a **gross** dollar. If all the dollars you bring into your household are **pretax** dollars, the government will get rich and you will stay poor.

The second kind of dollar is the **after tax** dollar. This is the dollar that people bring home in their paychecks. This dollar may be worth only 85 cents, or 72 cents, or 69 cents depending on which federal income tax bracket you fall into. If your state also has an income tax, your **after tax** dollar will decline even more. Thus, if your state has a 3% flat rate income tax, your **after tax** dollar will be worth only 82 cents, or 69 cents, or 66 cents, depending on your tax bracket.

In addition to income taxes, you must deduct social security taxes. Technically, these are not taxes, but you might as well think of them that way and include them in your calculations. At the moment, if you earn $53,400 or less at a wage earning job, you will pay 7.65% of every dollar you earn for social security withholding. If you work for yourself, you pay nearly double that amount. For the sake of simplicity,

I will round this 7.65% up to the next cent, and make it 8 cents out of every dollar are withheld for social security payments.

Now, after you have paid federal income tax, state income tax and social security, your **after tax dollar** is worth:

CALCULATION	Bracket #1	Bracket #2	Bracket #3
	$1.00	$1.00	$1.00
Subtract Federal taxes	.15	.28	.31
Subtract state income taxes	.03	.03	.03
Subtract SS withholding	.08	.08	.08
YOUR AFTER TAX DOLLAR IS WORTH:	.74	.61	.58

As shown above, depending upon which tax bracket you fall into, your **after tax** dollar is worth $.74, or $.61, or $.56.

The third kind of dollar is the most valuable kind: the **tax exempt, after tax,** or **non taxable dollar.** In the preceding chapter, I said that when you do jobs yourself at home, you create **after tax or non taxable dollars.** Although you cannot see them, you cannot hold them in your hand, you have created dollars which the government cannot tax. When you earn $30 at your job, you really have earned only about $20 in take home money, depending on your tax bracket. On the other hand, when you earn $30 at home, doing-it-yourself, you really have earned $30 full dollars, whether you can see them or not.

These dollars cannot be taxed by the federal government, or the state government, nor are they subject to social security withholding. This dollar is worth more than a **pretax** dollar. It is a dollar worth 100 cents plus the amount of your tax bracket. Thus, if you are in the 15% tax bracket, a **tax exempt** dollar is worth about $1.15. If you are in the 28% bracket, a **tax exempt** dollar is worth $1.28. If you are in the 31% tax bracket, a **tax exempt** is worth $1.31.

Then there is a **tax deferred** dollar. This is a dollar where the taxes are not taken out until some future date, when, hopefully, you will be in a lower tax bracket and not have to pay as much tax as you would have to pay today.

When making financial decisions, you need to remember these four different kinds of dollars. Throughout this book, calculations and comments will be made in terms of **pretax, after tax, tax exempt (non taxable), and tax deferred** dollars.

The important thing to remember is that every piece of income you earn at a paying job outside the home is subject to federal and state income taxes, and social security withholding until you earn more than $53,400. Every dollar that is paid to you by a bank as interest is a **pretax** dollar. You must pay taxes on that dollar, when it then becomes an **after tax** dollar, worth approximately between 15% and 31% less than when you first received it.

Every dollar that you spend on consumer goods and services is an **after tax dollar.** By the time you get that dollar, you've lost between 15% and 31% or more of its value due to tax withholding. If you spend this **after tax dollar** on **short term** consumption, you have wasted virtually every cent of that dollar.

So the economic job you face is to convert every dollar you earn to a **tax exempt or non taxable dollar.** You need to think constantly in terms of downshifting your dollars from **gross** dollars to **after tax** dollars to **tax deferred** dollars to **tax exempt or non taxable** dollars--the best dollars of all. There are only two primary ways for you make this shift among dollars. First, you can trade services rather than paying money for them. You baby sit for your neighbor and your neighbor baby sits for you. You swap worn out children's clothing.

The second way to earn **tax exempt or non taxable dollars** is to provide the goods or services for yourself without paying money for them: in other words, *do-it-yourself.* If you provide goods and services to yourself through your own labor, you have earned a **tax exempt** dollar. This is a dollar that does not show up as being paid to you, but you have earned it as surely as if you received it as salary. This is the richest, most valuable kind of dollar because it is **non taxable.**

You cannot earn **tax exempt dollars** by working for an employer. You cannot earn them by saving money in a bank. Interest is fully taxable. And **tax exempt dollars** are not money that has been paid to you by someone else but which you have decided not to report as income. That's tax evasion and punishable by law.

There is a third way to earn **tax exempt dollars**: investment in tax exempt bonds. I do not intend to discuss tax exempt investments in this book. You can learn more about tax exempt investments from any book or magazine that discusses investments in stocks and bonds. However, there is one point I'd like to make about tax exempt investments. They provide a tax break for wealthy people who have accumulated enough **capital** to invest in them. The average little guy puts his money into a bank savings account and gets socked with income taxes. This is an example of why it is so important for you to save that first chunk of money so you can begin to invest in the stock market and other investments where you can find **tax deferred and tax exempt** earnings. It's a harsh truth, but a truth nonetheless: our economy is set up so that those people who are richest continue to get richer, while those people who are poor will stay poor. The only way out of this trap is to accumulate **capital.**

Therefore, I will try to help you begin to think about every financial decision you make in terms of whether this decision creates **pretax** income, **after tax** income, **tax deferred income, or tax exempt** income.

There is a fifth factor that affects the value of a dollar: the **inflation rate.** In any given year, the value of the dollar decreases by the **rate of inflation.** In Russia recently, the value of their currency was declining by 25 percent a year. In terms of dollars, that means that at the end of the year, every dollar had lost 25 cents in purchasing power. In the United States recently, the rate of inflation has been quite low -- between 1% and 3% depending on how you estimate it.

When making some financial decisions, it is important to calculate in the inflation rate and its effect upon your dollars. For example, let's say you have $1,000 and you put it into a savings account which pays you 4% interest per year. Taking into consideration everything we have talked about above, you will recognize that in order to deposit $1,000 into a savings account, if you are working at a job outside the home, you will have had to earn:

1) $1,260 if you are in the 15% tax bracket ($1,000 plus $150 for federal income taxes, plus $30 for state income taxes plus $80 for social security withholding rough estimates); or

2) $1,390 if you are in the 28% bracket ($1,000 plus $280 for federal income taxes, plus 3% for state income taxes plus 8% for social security withholding).

Note: these figures are estimates, but they give you the idea. The figures above are the **gross income or pretax** income necessary to earn before you have $1,000 to deposit, **after taxes.** They are your poorest dollar.

Now, your bank pays about 4% a year interest on your $1,000, which comes to $40.00. If you are in the lowest tax bracket, you will have to pay about 15% income tax and let's assume 3% state income tax on that money. So, subtract 18% of $40.00, which comes to $7.20, leaving you with $32.80 profit on your investment of $1,000. Now, if the inflation rate for that year has been 3%, you should subtract $1.20 from the value of your $32.80, which leaves you with *real income* or profit of $31.60 on your $1,000 investment for a year.

CALCULATIONS:

$1,000 x .04 = $40.00 interest per year paid by your bank on a savings account.
$40.00 x .15 (your federal income tax rate) = $6.00 to be subtracted from your $40.
$40.00 x .03 (estimated state income tax rate) = $1.20 to be subtracted from your $40.

CHAPTER THREE: DOES IT PAY TO GET A JOB?

When does it make sense to work outside the home at a paying job and when does it make more sense to stay home? Both are *paying jobs*, but you need to know which job pays more, not only in money but in other values. If you do not now work outside the home for wages, recognize that your time spent working in your home is a *paying job.* It is, or it can be if you approach it with this idea in mind. As discussed earlier, the time you spend cooking, sewing, and doing house repairs earns you significant **non taxable** wages. Notice I do not include house cleaning in this list. I think most house cleaning is a very uneconomical use of one's time, and nine times out of ten you could be spending your time in some other more valuable or certainly more enjoyable way.

Outside of the home, perhaps the most important use of the **time versus money** concept occurs in one's job. If you work outside the home, you will be spending more than one third of each day and perhaps as much as one half of your entire life at a paying job. It makes good sense to insure that every hour of your labor on the job is as financially rewarding as possible.

Throughout this book, we've been talking about money, but we've also been talking about life's values. How you choose to spend your time should reflect what you think is important in your life: your moral and ethical values. But too many people get caught up in mindless tasks, idiot work, and futile running around which wastes their lives. I am urging you to use your money wisely so that you can spend more of your life on those activities and tasks that enhance your life on this planet.

Your job outside your home involves both money and values. Obviously if you derive pleasure from your job, you may be willing to accept lower pay in return for this enjoyment. Nonetheless, pleasure in your work should not stop you from earning as much money per hour of work as possible.

When thinking of a job, you need to ask yourself why it is necessary for you to get a paying job outside the home? If you are single, widowed, or divorced, the answer is obvious: you have no other source of income.

For married women, the answer is less obvious. If you are married, you may be pressured to go out into the work force, to get a "real" job. Many husbands urge their wives to "go out and get a job" to bring in extra income. Nowadays many married women work because their husbands cannot find jobs or are in jobs that are not secure. Thus, compared with thirty years ago, it is common for women to work outside the home. More than half of married women do.

Another reason for a married woman to work outside the home is that if you are ever left alone, either through divorce or the death of your spouse, your years as a housewife will be held against you when you go out to look for a full time, wage earning job. Your years out of the work force will almost automatically insure that you will only be able to get a very low paying job. It therefore makes sense to work at a paying job so that you know you can always support yourself financially. It provides you with an employment history, and it also provides you with your own social security payments when you retire.

In addition to money, there are important psychological reasons for getting a job outside the home. First among them is that you want to do it. You prefer working at a paying job rather than staying at home. You like the challenge, the social contacts, the sense of accomplishment.

Working outside the home will change the power games in your marriage. I have a friend who is currently in an unhappy marriage. She has a young son, now about ten years old. Her husband taunts her that she is dependent on him, that he controls the purse strings, and that he can leave her any time he feels like it. At last she decided she must go into the full time work force, which she has done. She decided that financial independence was important not only for her own psychological well being, but important for her son's. She did not want him to continually witness a woman being verbally abused and made to crawl by a man. She did not think this kind of role modeling would help her son become a caring, thoughtful man. She writes that she delights in being able to purchase things for her home that her husband would not allow before: flowering cherry trees and dogwoods for her yard among other things. She enjoys the challenge of her job and the thrill of developing new skills.

On the other hand, if you are married and have children, there are many advantages to staying at home rather than working outside the home, advantages on which society cannot (or does not) place a dollar value. For example, my former neighbor was a full time housewife. Nearly every day she walked to the school bus stop, about a quarter of a mile from her home, to meet her children. She used the walk back home as a time to talk with her kids about their days at school, their problems with teachers, fellow students, their homework. She used this time to establish communications with her children, an absolutely essential link with them as they grew into young adulthood.

She used her time at home to supervise the homework of her children, making sure that they did it, did it well, and did it on time. If there were problems at school, she did not hesitate to go see the teachers, the principal, the coaches to insure that her children were getting the best possible education in a supportive environment. Her daughter is now in a major Ivy League college majoring in biology. Her son was recently cited in the local newspaper for his superior sportsmanship and ice hockey skills, his willingness to work "for the team" rather than solely for his own self glory.

I cannot emphasize enough how valuable to your family and to society this work is. It is irreplaceable work. Unfortunately, society does not wish to pay women for this work, and women who have spent their entire lives at home, raising children, often end up as the poorest members of society: the "displaced homemakers".

When women choose to work outside the home, they assume that they can earn more money at a job than by staying at home. This assumption needs to be examined. It is not always true.

To begin with, many women work for very low wages, and by the time the expenses associated with their job are subtracted, they really take home very little real money. I shall go through the **hidden costs** associated with working in a moment.

Secondly, for most women, going out to work means that instead of holding down one job, they now hold down two jobs: the one at the office and the usual one at home. As a rule, husbands still do not significantly help their wives with housework and child care. Single women or unmarried women with children definitely hold down two jobs with no help from anyone else in the household.

If you are already working at a job outside the home or you wish to get a job, how can you be sure that you are actually earning more money at your job than you could save by staying at home? How can you determine that your job is really worth the time you spend at it?

There are three things you need to examine. First, the actual wages you are being paid. You want to earn as much per hour as is possible. If you can earn $20 an hour at a job, this is much better than earning $5 an hour. But wages are only the tip of the iceberg when it comes to determining which one job pays more than another, or whether a job pays more than the money you save by working full time at home.

Besides wages, you need to examine the **hidden costs** of working at that job. These costs need to be subtracted from the wages you earn at that job. What are some of the **hidden cost** associated with a paying job?

Hidden Costs:

If you are married and you get a job, it may force your household into a higher tax bracket. At the moment, there are three major federal income tax brackets: 15%, 28% and 31%. The breaks for these brackets are:

Type of Household		
Married filing jointly	15%	$1.00-$36,900
	28%	up to $89,150
	31%	up to $140,00
Single	15%	up to $22,100
	28%	up to 53,500
	31%	up to $115,000

Married filing separately	15%	$1.00 - $18,450
	28%	up to $44,575
	31%	up to $70,000
Single head of household	15%	$1.00 - $29,600
	28%	up to $76,400
	31%	up to $127,500

If your husband earns $35,000 a year and you get a job that pays $15,000 a year, chances are you will find yourself in the 28% tax bracket instead of the 15% tax bracket. This means, for every additional dollar above $36,900 that you bring in, you and your husband will pay 28 cents of it to the federal government instead of 15 cents. This is a rough approximation, but paying an additional 13 cents in federal taxes for each dollar you earn above $36,900 household income should be added into the costs associated with your working outside the home. You should also include any state income taxes where you live.

Another **hidden cost** in addition to state and federal income taxes, is social security withholding, which is 7.65% up to the first $53,400 you earn. On a salary of $15,000, you will pay $1,147.50 in social security withholding per year. It is true that you will receive some of this money back when you retire, but you should figure it into the costs of holding a job.

You will also have withheld a small amount for unemployment compensation taxes.

Besides taxes, another **hidden cost** is transportation to and from your job. You may be forced to buy another car or a better car. Cars cost a lot of money, every day. Let's assume that it will cost you $10 a day in transportation costs to get to a job. For a 20 day work month, you will spend 20 days x $10 = $200 for transportation each month.

Your wardrobe can be a **hidden job cost**. On your job, you may have to look more professional and well dressed than you would at home. You may feel that you must have your hair done more frequently to maintain an appropriate appearance. A recent article in "Working Woman" (as quoted in *The Denver Post*, Friday October 30, 1992) reported that 62% of their respondents to a poll paid from $100 to $300 for one work outfit. Twenty-three percent said they spend less than $100, and 11% said they spend from $300 - $500 per outfit. Let's assume that you will spend about $150 a month additionally on clothing, hair care, and dry cleaning bills. By clothing I include hosiery, undergarments, shoes, handbags, scarves, jewelry and other accessories in addition to the basic suit or dress. This also includes coats and jackets, as well as rain gear and umbrellas.

If you have young children, you will pay day care expenses. Let's assume that you will pay $75 per week for daycare for one child. That comes to $300 a month for daycare.

Now, add up these expenses to find your costs of getting a $15,000 a year job:

Potential Hidden Job Costs:

Item	Cost
Federal income taxes (estimated $3,000 per year) /12 months = per month	$250.00
Social Security withholding, $1140 per year/12 months - per month	$95.63
Estimated car expenses per month	$200.00
Estimated clothing, hair, care, personal care expenses per month	$150.00
Day care per month for one child	$300.00
Total Estimated Job Costs Per Month	**$995.63**

A job that pays you $15,000 per year gross (**gross income means income before any deductions for taxes or insurance or social security have been withheld,**) will pay you $1,250.00 per month.

Subtract your job related expenses of $995.63 from your $1,250.00 and you will have actually earned only $254.37 profitable wages for your 160 hours of labor, (4 weeks x 40 hours) or $1.59 per hour additional real income or profit after subtracting your expenses.

We have not included the additional costs of lunches and coffee breaks. These are real expenses unless you bring your own lunches and coffee. They can easily add another $5 a day to your job related expenses, or another $100 a month. If we add these expenses into the figures above, your real net income for 160 hours of labor is only $154.37 per month or 96 cents an hour or about $8 a day.

Another **hidden cost** to be factored in is your time to and from your job. An average commute is about a half hour each way, or an hour a day out of your life just for travel time, and most companies do not pay for this time. Yet, it is time taken out of your life.

A further consideration is whether your job gives you paychecks weekly, bi-weekly or monthly. If you are paid weekly or bi-weekly, you will receive a paycheck for every week of the year. If you are paid *monthly*, you effectively give your employer four weeks of your labor for free. This occurs because there are 52 weeks in a year, but our calendars show only 12 months instead of 13 four week months. To make up for this aberration, calendar months have more than 28 days in them. Thus, if you are paid on Fridays, about every three months, one month arrives with five Friday pay days in it instead of four. There will be four months in the year with five Fridays in them. If you are paid weekly, you will get five paychecks that month, which can provide some savings benefits as I will discuss in the chapter on Budgets. If you are paid monthly, this extra pay day signals that you have worked an extra week for free.

The third thing you need to look at beyond wages and costs associated with the job are **fringe benefits**. Two jobs paying $15,000 a year can differ greatly in their fringe benefits and thus their real value to you as a wage earner. Often the **fringe benefits** are worth more to you than your actual salary. **Fringe benefits** are not usually taxed at the full rate as are wages, and some benefits are **tax exempt** or **tax deferred.** Listed below are typical **benefits** that companies or organizations can provide to their employees in addition to salary. NOTE: These benefits usually only apply to full-time employees. Part-time employees are almost always excluded from receiving these kinds of benefits. This is one way that corporations cut their costs: they increase their hiring of part-time employees so they don't have to pay as much in benefits. If you must work outside the home, try not to work part-time unless you also receive benefits plus salary.

Common Fringe Benefits in Addition to Wages

Medical insurance
Dental insurance
Insurance for eye care
Group life insurance
Long term disability insurance
Time off for illness
Vacation days and holidays
Personal leave for other reasons than your illness (child care or care of an aging adult relative)
Pensions and retirement plans
Stock purchase plans
Legal insurance
Salary bonuses
Tuition for your further education or that of your children

Medical plans vary widely, and many companies are cutting back on the amount of medical care their plans will cover. They are increasing the amounts that employees have to pay for medical insurance. When you interview for a job, you should determine exactly what these medical benefits will be and compare them from job to job. You will need to know what part of your medical insurance you must pay for yourself, if any. With the rising costs of medical insurance in this country, finding a job that will pay at least some part of your medical insurance is one of the best investments of your time you can make.

Next to medical insurance and long-term disability insurance, I regard pension plans as the most important part of any job package, and 401 (k) plans as the best type of pension or retirement plan. These retirement plans allow employees to save as much as 6% of their gross income up to a maximum of $8,728 a year. Employees do not pay any taxes on this money until they withdraw it. In other words, you get to save with **pretax dollars**. The money invested in your pension grows **tax deferred.** You do not pay income taxes on the interest earned until you withdraw the money after you retire. The money is invested in a variety of ways including money market accounts and stock funds. If you were to invest $500 each month in a 401 (k) plan growing at a rate of 8% per year, you would have $475,500 saved in twenty-five years.

Compare this with the average savings account. You have to put your **after tax** money into the savings account, where you may receive 4% interest on it, which you will have to pay taxes on at the end of each year.

Some companies offer traditional pensions wholly paid for by the company. Some companies pay partial pensions.

If you are going to spend the best part of your life and your waking hours working, it pays to find a job that not only pays a decent salary, but pays significant portions of your medical care and pension costs.

If you are married to a wage earning husband who is covered by medical insurance and retirement plans, for you to work for $15,000 a year or less at a company that does not pay any or all of these benefits is "economically" almost a complete waste of your time.

When considering an outside the home job, you should add up the costs of taking that job and subtract them from the *salary plus benefits.* This will give you the actual wage per hour that you are bringing home. You do not have to be completely precise in your calculations. Rough estimates will do, but try to be as accurate as you can. The important thing to remember is that: taking a job costs money, and it should not cost you more money to work than you are bringing home in salary plus benefits.

If you are married with children, you can probably earn more money staying at home and using your at-home time wisely. If your estimated job costs subtracted from your gross wages show that you are actually earning only $8 a day, you can surely earn more than that staying at home.

As I mentioned above, there are non-economic advantages to taking a wage earning job, and many women must start somewhere, even if that means in a low paying job. If you do take a low paying job without benefits, try to find one that offers you opportunities for career advancement or that offers a variety of in-house training programs to its employees to continually improve and upgrade skills. Try to get that job as close to your home as possible to lower your transportation costs.

I started my life as a typist and worked my way up to being a secretary by studying shorthand at home at night. At one time in my life, I faced a choice between two jobs. The first job paid $100 a week and gave me four weeks of paid vacation time. The second job paid only $95 a week and gave me only two weeks of paid vacation. At the last minute, purely on a hunch, I took that second job because the people that I had interviewed were interesting and energetic. The building seemed "to jump" inside. I made this decision in complete ignorance of what either job entailed, but I quickly learned that the job I had taken offered an opportunity to become a professional market researcher. The other job would have kept me as a secretary for my life.

Now, do not believe for an instant that this opportunity for career advancement was handed to me on a platter. I had to overcome serious obstacles to get on the research staff, obstacles of being a female, having a degree from a western university rather than an Ivy League college, and the obstacle of being such a good secretary that no one wanted to promote me to the research staff. Secretaries were harder to find. However, I finally made the jump onto the professional staff, and my income, self esteem and opportunity to broaden every aspect of my life blossomed.

It took me a year and a half to get onto the research staff (and I needed the "pull" of one of the male vice presidents to finally get me the job). Then it took me another ten years to reach vice president. Many men made this transition more rapidly. Nonetheless, I still feel I was extremely lucky to have fallen into that profession and to have had the chance, difficult as it was, to create a new life for myself through this company's "opportunity for advancement."

Companies often promise women that they will have "opportunities for advancement", and after a few months on the job, you will learn that this is a lie. When you interview for a job, really search into whether such opportunities exist, what you would have to do to advance, and does that organization have training programs or does it fund your tuition and provide time for you to train for advancement at nearby schools or colleges. Ask to talk with other women on the staff who have advanced from a low level job into a higher level, professional job. Find out what they have to say about "opportunities to advance". This particular **fringe benefit** may outweigh any other benefits and certainly, for the short term, can offset a lower salary.

I have a friend who was a practicing nurse for twenty years. She could not tolerate the profession any longer. She was fed up with the long hours, the work over holidays, the condescending attitude of the doctors around her. She found a job using a "headhunter" or a search firm, as a technical writer for a major pharmaceutical firm. This firm provided training for her in this new job, and in addition the company promised to pay her tuition to college so she could get her master's degree. Unfortunately, she learned that her supervisor would not allow her to plan her schedule to attend classes. She was forced to travel several days a week out of town, which kept her from attending classes regularly. Still she continued to take classes until finally, in desperation and anger, she quit her job. She had saved enough money to continue her classes for another three months, when she finally got her master's degree. She sold her house and moved to the Chesapeake Bay area. She now works at a lower paying job, but she works in an environment that is less expensive, one that provides the amenities she wanted: boating, bicycling, a slower way of life.

For this woman the chance to get her master's degree, paid for by the company for which she worked, offset all the other benefits and hassles of that job. For a year or two she had to work double time--time at her job and time to complete her college educationbut she did it.

One further asset to holding a wage earning job: if your job does not provide you with a pension, you may be entitled to deposit money into an Individual Retirement Account. You are eligible if you are not covered by an employer pension, or if you are single and earning an adjusted gross income of less than $35,000 a year, or if you are married and together you and your husband earn less than $50,000 a year.

An IRA may be the only opportunity you have for accumulating **capital**. You can deduct the $2,000 maximum per year that you save from your federal income taxes, and the money in your IRA earns interest **tax deferred** until you withdraw it on your retirement. You do not have to deposit the full $2,000 per year, but if you can, it is one of the better ways for ordinary people to save for their retirements if they are not covered by a pension where they work.

It takes work to learn the rules governing an IRA: where you can invest it, and the tax rules affecting it. However, it is time well spent for the average woman.

Throughout this chapter I have compared the value of working at home versus the value of working outside the home. For many women, working at home is the best use, the most economic use of their time, but that assumes that these women are *actually working* at home and not sitting on their duffs watching Soaps on TV.

What kinds of jobs earn you money while at home? Cooking, sewing, home repairs are the most obvious. Perhaps the next most important one is to educate yourself by studying the personal financial sections of the magazines and newspapers to learn how to invest your money to earn more money.

Keeping track of your checking account balances; paying off all your bills promptly. Taking advantage of any money saving programs offered to people in your income category, such as homestead rebates. Learning the tax laws so you can better keep track of your own income tax records, deductions, and file your own tax returns. Filling out your own tax returns saves you quite a bit of money, but only if you know what you are doing and make no mistakes. If your children are getting ready for college, searching out the scholarships and financial aid that might be available to them.

Studying nutrition and home health care to keep your family in good health at lower costs with fewer visits to the doctor. Planting a large vegetable garden and either freezing or canning the food from that garden to feed your family.

Another way you can earn money for yourself is to attend local school board meetings and local government meetings to insure a continued delivery of high quality education and civic services to your neighborhood. If you own your home, keeping your neighborhood in good repair is a very valuable use of your time because it will maintain or increase the value of your house. Making sure your schools deliver the best education enhances your neighborhood and also assures that your own children will be well prepared to go out into the world to make their own way.

Besides these types of informal education, one of the best ways to increase your economic value while at home is to take courses to advance your formal schooling. Either attend adult education classes, vocational classes, classes to finish your high school degree, or classes to obtain a college degree. Besides making your life more enjoyable, the more education you have completed, the better your chances of obtaining a higher paying job.

Recent census data indicate that **median incomes** (the median is that point where half the population earns less and half earn more) increase substantially with educational achievement.

Women ages 25-34 years	**Yearly Income**
High school completed	$17,559.00
Bachelor's degree	$27,097.00
Master's degree	$31,465.00

Women ages 35-44 years

High school completed	$18,940.00
Bachelor's degree	$30,836.00
Master's degree	$34,455.00

Women ages 45-54

High school completed	$19,231.00
Bachelor's degree	$31,462.00
Master's degree	$36,686.00

Our economy is changing, and the types of jobs available are also changing. In the past, factory union jobs paid high wages, good benefits and demanded less education. Nowadays, the new jobs being created demand more and more education. High paying jobs that do not demand high education levels are disappearing. All that remain for the poorly educated are low paying service jobs--waiters and waitresses, unskilled hotel/motel laborers, health care service jobs.

Besides money, however, education rewards you in many ways. It opens new areas of intellectual interest and challenge in art, literature, science. When you have more education, you become an interesting person because you have so many more things you know about and are interested in.

When I was younger, I did not want to go to college. My mother told me, "I don't care whether you go more than one year or not, but you will go to see what is there, and then if you decide to drop out, you will know what you have missed." I did not go to college to learn a skill that would earn me money. I studied art. Once again, my mother insisted that "A good education leads to a richer life." And it has. Not an easier life, but a richer life.

SECTION TWO: SPENDING YOUR MONEY EFFECTIVELY

CHAPTER FOUR: INTEREST RATE SPREADS

I have urged you to think of money as a commodity like any other commodity, such as pork bellies or corn or wheat. Because money is a commodity, people who lend money charge interest for it. Because money is a commodity, you should try to earn interest on whatever money you have in your possession. **Interest is money earned by money.** You pay interest on the money you borrow, and you earn interest on money you save or invest. The purpose of this chapter is to help you learn to handle your money so that it earns interest for *you* instead of earning money for a store, a bank, or some other institution.

Most people think that the only place they can earn interest on their money is in a bank savings account or from some sort of investment in stocks or bonds. In fact, you can earn interest on your money by not paying interest (or fees, which are the same thing) to a bank, a store, or some other institution for the use of their money.

Let's look at some common interest rates as of today (April, 1995). I will list the highest yield in each category:

Money market account--5.89%
Six month certificate of deposit--6.50%
One year certificate of deposit--7.09%
Five year certificate of deposit--7.61%

(Source: *Money,* April 1995, p. 47.)

These are the rates you could earn on your money if you put it into a bank for savings.

Now, let's look at how much interest you can *pay* when you use your credit cards and do not pay off the entire balance each month. The rates below are for various MasterCard/Visa cards charging the *lowest* interest rates in the country at this time:

Lowest rate 8.75% - 10.20%
Average rate among all credit cards 18.0%

My own credit card charges me 18.40% per year, up from 15.90% annual percentage rate two years ago.

If we subtract the amount of interest you could earn in some sort of savings account--let's say 5%--from the amount you could be paying on your charge cards--let's say 18%--you have an **interest rate spread** of 13%. You need to manipulate **interest rate spreads** to your financial advantage. This is called **arbitraging**, a word that I happen to love just for its own sake.

The **interest rate spread** between what you can earn on your savings and what you pay for goods and services you buy on credit is one way the American economy takes unfair advantage of both savers and those consumers who use credit. If you also add in the fact that you must pay income taxes on the interest you earn on your savings, but that you no longer get a tax deduction for the interest you pay on your debts (except on a home mortgage or a home equity loan), this basic unfairness of the economy becomes even more pronounced.

By paying very low rates on savings, the average household is encouraged not to save, but to spend. After all, putting $1,000 in a 5% certificate of deposit only yields $50 per year, **pretax.** After you subtract about 25% on average for income taxes, your actual money earned is only $37.50. In the earlier chapter on **pretax and after tax dollars,** I showed you how little money you actually earn by putting money in a savings account or CD. No wonder people in this country do not bother to save money.

However, if you buy things on credit and do *not* pay off your charge account balances each month, you are paying nearly 20% more on the price of everything you purchase. Thus, if your charge card average balance for a year is $2,200, which is typical, you will pay approximately $396 a year in interest charges.

These interest rate charges wipe out any profits you might make from taking advantage of a so-called "sale." Notice that I have not added in the yearly fees for owning the card, which can run as much as $35 a year.

If you have an average outstanding balance of $1,000 on your credit card at 18% interest, you are paying about $180 a year interest charges. However if you pay off this balance, you have actually "earned" money at a rate of 18% a year.

Revolving charge accounts eat up your hard earned money. For example, my recent credit card bill is $491.38. Let's say it's $500 to make things easier to calculate. I am told that I only need to repay $14 this month on that balance, and everything will be OK. So let's say I pay only $14 instead of paying off the entire balance. During the next month, interest will be charged on the remaining balance of $486 at the rate of 1.65%. That means in one month I will pay $8.01 interest. This will be added to my balance so that next month I will owe money on $486 + $8.01 = $494.01. If I have charged any additional purchases, this amount is automatically added into my balance, and interest rate charges are applied to the total new balance. If I only pay $14 a month on my balance, I am paying *interest on interest.*

The moral of this story is that you must absolutely learn to *pay off your charge account balances in full* every month if you are ever to have surplus money. This is one of the most effective ways of spending your money. Failure to pay off charge account balances is the easiest way to routinely *lose* money. You might as well take your hard earned cash and throw it out on the streets.

It is worth whatever it takes for you to save up that first $1,000 in cash so that you will always have enough money on hand to pay off your credit card balances each month before any interest is charged. If you have $1,000 in a savings account earning 4% and you have a charge account balance of $1,000 on which you are paying 18%, it saves you money --$151.20 to be exact -- to pay off that balance. This is **interest** that you have in effect paid to yourself, and it is **after tax** interest. You do not have to pay taxes on money that you save this way.

An example of the powerful negative effect of high interest rates on purchases occurs most spectacularly among those people who "rent to buy." Many people cannot afford to pay the full price for a washing machine, dryer, sofa or TV, so they "rent to buy." They put a small amount down on the object, and then pay for it over a period of several months. While the monthly payments are small, the interest charges that are packed into that monthly charge add up to substantial amounts of money and inflate the actual costs of the object purchased.

Recently I priced out a washer/dryer at a "rent to buy" store and a similar washer/ dryer on sale at Sears. The rent-to-buy price was $15.95 per week for 104 weeks: This comes to an actual cost of:

<u>CALCULATION:</u>
$15.95 per week x 104 weeks = $1,658.80 for the washer and dryer at the rent-to-buy.

The price at Sears was $718 for the pair when you paid cash for them. Subtract $718 from $1,658.80 to find a difference of $940.80 for the same two objects: a washer and dryer!

You can see how important it is to save up your money to buy such items paying cash immediately. The American credit economy keeps poor people poor. They pay twice as much for the things they buy because they do not have the available cash. Rather than use a "rent-to-buy" store, people would be much better off to save that $15 a week in a cookie jar until they have the cash necessary to pay for a washer and dryer on the spot.

A woman who once worked for me wanted to buy a dryer on a rent-to-buy contract. I was horrified. I suggested that she simply string a clothesline in her apartment and hang her wash there during the day. She wasn't at home during the day, so it didn't matter if the living room was full of laundry.

This is a perfect example of paying for convenience: the convenience of owning a dryer versus the inconvenience of hanging wash outdoors or in the apartment. The clothesline and clothes pins cost a few dollars. It is true, she had to lug her wet laundry home from the Laundromat in a laundry cart and then hang it up to dry. This is hard work, but by doing this for one year, she is in a position to pay cash for a dryer and avoid paying twice as much for a dryer as it is actually worth.

The American economy encourages you to want things, and to want them NOW! It's the NOW that will keep you broke. People buy on their charge accounts or on rent-to-buy contracts so that they can have things without waiting. This urge to have things immediately keeps people poor. You must discipline yourself to postpone purchases as long as possible, until you have the money to pay cash for them, or pay for them within the 25 days allowed on most credit cards before interest is charged.

I priced a 20" TV at the rent-to-buy and one at Sears.

CALCULATION:
The rent-to-own was $11 per week for 18 months or
78 weeks x $11 = $858.

A similar TV at Sears was $289.99 or $568.01 less.

You can see from the numbers above exactly how one decision -- to rent-to-buy or to pay using revolving credit -- can eat up your valuable money and give you nothing in return except immediate gratification.

One area, however, where credit is a boon to Americans is that mortgages allow them to buy houses. Here again interest rate spreads should be examined. Right now, mortgage rates are very low. Nonetheless, you are paying interest month after month for the use of that mortgage money lent by the bank. That means that over the lifetime of your mortgage you can pay for your house two or three times over.

CALCULATION:
If you have a 30 year mortgage of $60,000 on your home at an interest rate of 8%, your monthly payment will be $440.26 per month, principle and interest per month.

> Multiply that monthly payment by 30 years x 12 months per year and you will have paid 360 months times $440.26 = $158,493.60 for your house instead of $60,000. In other words you have paid nearly three times the original mortgage for your house.

You save big bucks if you carry a fifteen year mortgage rather than a thirty year mortgage. Compare what happens if you have a $100,000 mortgage on your home for 30 years versus one for 15 years. For a 7% thirty year mortgage loan, you would pay a total of $139,760 **interest.** For a 7% fifteen year mortgage loan, you would pay a total of $61,820 **interest.** The monthly payment varies by $233 a month: $899 for the fifteen year mortgage versus $666 for the thirty year mortgage. By digging up that additional $233 a month for a fifteen year mortgage, you save yourself **$61,820** on the cost of your house.

In the early years of a mortgage, most of your monthly payment is **interest**. Therefore, economically you can save thousands of dollars if you pay additional **principle** on your mortgage each month. On a $75,000 loan at 10% for 30 years, if you pay an additional $54.85 per month on your payment, you will save $57,000 off your total mortgage costs. (Source: "Straight Talk on Your Money," December, 1992, p. 9.)

Some financial advisors may say not to pay off your mortgage early, especially at the current low interest rates. They recommend taking the money you would use to pay off an 8% mortgage and investing it in mutual funds that are now yielding about 10%. This is playing an interest rate spread. To do this demands personal discipline on your part, and I don't recommend it unless you are very confident of your stock market investing skills. It takes no investment skill to pay off your mortgage. That is a solid investment in saving money. While you are paying off your mortgage, you can study the stock market so that when you finally have the money available, you will also have the knowledge. Meanwhile, prepay your mortgage.

The basic strategy with **interest rate spreads** is to try to get them to work to your advantage rather than against you. That means, paying as little for credit as possible and earning as much for your savings as possible. Playing **interest rate spreads** leads to home equity loans, which make good economic sense but only if you do not use them to constantly finance further short term consumption.

At this time, home equity loans charge in the range of 7 1/2% to about 8% interest. These loan rates could go as high as 18% depending on the level of interest rates (the prime rate) in the economy as a whole, but right now, home equity rates and home mortgage rates have fallen to their lowest levels in many years. If you have credit card balances of $2,000, on which you are paying 18% interest, it makes sense to use your home equity line of credit (another good reason for trying to own your home rather than renting) to pay off your credit card balances. Let's do some arithmetic.

CALCULATION:
Credit card balance $2,000 per year x 18% = $360 simple interest per year.
Home equity credit $2,000 per year x 8%= $160 interest per year.

As the above shows, you could save $200 a year in simple interest by using your home equity loan to pay off your credit card balance. Furthermore, on a home equity loan, the Federal government lets you deduct the interest, so you can add a tax deduction if you are in the 28% bracket of $44.80, which means that in fact you are paying only $115.20 interest instead of $360.00 on a loan of $2,000.

CALCULATION:
$2,000 x 8% interest rate = $160
Multiply $160 x .28% federal tax rate = 44.80.
Subtract $44.80 from $160 to get $115.20 total interest paid **after tax**.

If you are in the 15% tax bracket, multiply $160 x .15 = $24.
Subtract $24 from $160 = $136 total interest paid on $2,000 loan **after tax.**

When you borrow money at a low rate of interest to pay off loans that cost a higher rate of interest, you are playing an **interest rate spread.** The major problem with home equity lines of credit is that if you let them get out of hand, using them only to pay for consumption, you might lose your home, and you are certainly losing the forced savings feature inherent in home ownership.

Keep in mind that no matter how clever you are in playing interest rate spreads, you are still *spending money*, and if you spend more money than you earn, or if you spend as much money as you earn, you remain poor.

In addition to interest rate plays used for consumption, there are interest rate plays used for savings. The most obvious is not keeping your money in a bank savings account, but investing it in a higher paying vehicle, such as mutual funds or annuities, or even U. S. Savings Bonds, which you can buy at your bank without paying any kind of brokerage fees.

When making any kind of investment the first rule of interest rates, or **rates of return** on your investments is that the HIGHER THE RATE OF RETURN, THE RISKIER YOUR INVESTMENT. When you read about investments paying 15% rates of return when savings accounts are paying only 4%, this large **interest rate spread** is a red flag warning you to be careful. When a company or financial institution or a public authority pays exceptionally high rates of return on their bonds or notes, it usually means that organization is in shaky financial condition.

Although I have talked in terms of **interest rate spreads,** I really want you to understand the concept that money is a commodity that can earn money for you when you save, or can cost you money when you borrow it by using credit. Therefore, you need to **comparison shop** to get the highest rates of return on money you save or invest. You need to **comparison shop** to get the lowest possible rates when you must borrow money.

In addition to **comparison shopping for rates**, you need to always evaluate those rates in terms of whether they involve **pretax, after tax, or tax exempt** dollars.

One way of playing an interest rate spread involves checking account fees. While **interest** is one way that money earns money, fees are another way that money earns money, only in this case, the bank is charging you fees and also using your money. Some credit cards may only charge you 14% interest, but they may also charge you a yearly fee of $35. Think of this as interest too. Any fee or interest charge is what you are paying to use someone else's money.

For example, my bank charges me $7.00 a month for my checking account unless I keep a minimum balance of $700 in it each month.

CALCULATION:
12 months of fees x $7 = $84 a year in checking account charges if I do not keep a minimum balance of $700 in it. This may be called a fee, but I see it as interest that the bank is charging me for providing a checking account.

If I keep $700 in my savings account, I earn:

$700 x 4% = $28 a year in interest, which is taxable at my federal rate of 31%, which means I actually earn only about $19 a year on my savings. ($28 x .31 = $8.68 subtracted from $28 = $19.32 after tax interest earned).

If I take that $700 out of savings and keep it in my checking account, I in effect earn $84 **tax exempt interest** a year -- $7 x 12 months = by not paying checking account fees. If I keep that $700 in my savings account, I earn only $19 **after tax** savings.

Thus, you can take advantage of a variety of "spreads" between what you must pay for money and what you can earn on the same money if you use it some other way. Just because you put money in your savings account does not necessarily mean that you are really saving money.

Managing money is a juggling act between your spending and your earning power. To earn the most from any given dollar, you need to constantly calculate the spreads. You need to compare the cost of money you use (fees and interest rates you pay) compared with the money you can earn or save on the same dollars by using them differently.

I have seen financial advice suggesting that people should move their savings accounts to such and such a bank because that bank pays 4.5 % interest instead of 4% interest. On $1,000, that one half percentage point only amounts to $5 a year, which may not even pay for the additional gas to drive to a different bank. Include the fact that the federal government and your state government will take their cut of taxes from this additional $5. It certainly does not compensate you for the time involved in changing banks. If it takes you an hour to fill out the new forms, your first year's interest has already been spent. This is a **time versus money** calculation you should make routinely.

When shopping for checking accounts and savings accounts, look not only at the interest rates being paid but on the fees being charged. Learn to manipulate your savings account and checking account balances to lower your fees. This creates **after tax** savings, which are greater than any **pretax** earnings of interest you may receive on the same amount of money.

Recently, my bank sent me a large brochure outlining the different checking accounts they offer. It took me about an hour to read this brochure while trying to figure out which checking account would be best for me. Roughly, the alternatives listed were:

<u>Regular Checking</u>
No service fee if $500 minumum balance is maintained.
$6.00 monthly fee if balance goes below $500.

<u>Money market checking</u>
No service fee if minimum balance of $1,000 is maintained.
$8.00 monthly fee if balance goes below $1,000.
Simple interest paid monthly on the cash in that account at current money market rates. At present, money market rates are about 3.25% on $1,000 or $32.50 a year, which is taxable to me in the 31% bracket, which leaves only about $22.00 per year real **after tax** interest received each year on a $1,000 balance in this account. That comes to $1.83 per month interest on $1,000.

Linked checking to any other account
No service fee if I maintain a total balance of $5,000 in CD's or other savings accounts. If my combined balance falls below the minimum, $9.00 service charge is assessed. Right now, current CD rates are about 4% depending on the time of the CD. 4% x $5,000 = $200 a year interest on the CD, or $16.66 per month, taxable to me in 31% bracket = $11.49 each month in real after tax interest received.

In example #1, by keeping $500 in my account, I save (earn) 12 x $6 monthly fee per month or $72.00 per year. This is **after tax** savings. If I put the same $500 into a 4% savings account, I earn $20 a year interest, on which I must pay 31% taxes, so that my **after tax interest** income is about $18. Obviously, it makes sense for me to keep the $500 in my checking account to save the $72 in fees rather than to put the same money into a savings account.

The same arithmetic applies to the other examples. If I keep $5,000 in some other savings account, I earn/save $9 per month checking account fees, which equals $108 a year **after tax** income. I am also earning about 4% interest on the $5,000 which comes to another $200 a year, but I must subtract 31% for income taxes, so my actual interest income is about $138.00 per year. Add $138.00 plus $108 in saved checking fees, and my total income is $246 for the year on that $5,000 kept in the bank, or about 4.9% **after tax interest** income.

Now, if I take that $5,000, keep $500 of it in a regular checking account and invest the remaining $4,500 in a mutual fund that pays a rate of return of about 9% a year, I earn $405, subject to 31% taxes = about $280 plus the $72 I've saved in checking account fees for a total **after tax** income of $352.00 -- an increase of about $100 above what I would earn if I kept the money in the bank. Actually, the tax rate on the mutual fund earnings may not be quite that high, and these figures do not allow for the fact that the mutual fund shares may increase in value during the year, giving me some **capital gains**, while the CD balance remains static. (My mutual fund shares might also decline.)

These calculations take time, but if I spend one hour doing this arithmetic, and save myself $100 for the year, don't you think that is a very good wage rate for the time spent? My $100 an hour earned at home is **after tax** income.

In addition to avoiding fees, one other advantage of keeping a minimum balance in one's checking account is that you can also avoid bounced checks. Recently I read that the average charge for returning a bounced check is about $18. It costs a bank about $1.50 to process a bounced check, so if your bank is charging you $18, the bank is earning a $16.50 profit for each bounced check.

In the earlier chapter I talked about making your home *your business*. Taking the time to calculate out interest rate spreads and fees on the money you save and the money you spend is one way of running your at-home business effectively. You earn significant money by taking the time to learn how to do this kind of work. The one hour spent calculating out your bank checking account charges could save you anywhere between $50 and $100 a year. Isn't spending this hour a better use of your time than watching the evening news on TV one night?

CHAPTER FIVE: CAPITAL--MONEY THAT MAKES MONEY

The United States is a capitalistic country. This means that if you wish to become wealthy, you must accumulate **capital**. One definition of **capital,** and the one I will use throughout this book is, "Any form of material wealth used or available for use in the production of more wealth." I am going to broaden this definition to include *any asset you own that you can use to make more money for yourself.*

In the earlier chapters, I have described ways that you can use your **labor** to make money by working effectively at home and finding the highest paying, most profitable types of jobs. However, if you depend solely on earning money by your **labor**, you will usually remain poor, or at least you won't get very rich. People think that the only way they can obtain money is to work for it, to get some wages, but the United States income tax system and our country's economy are set up in such a way that for the average American, simply earning wages will never increase that person's wealth. To become really wealthy, you must accumulate **capital** -- assets that produce money for you without your having to work; assets that produce money for you while you are sleeping.

Thus, in thinking about how you *spend* your money, you need to divide your personal property into assets that *produce* money for you and possessions which are sometimes considered assets but which *drain* money away from you. You want to spend as much of your income as possible on **capital assets** that will earn money for you while you sleep. You want to spend as little money as possible on things that end up simply costing you more money. Most people run their households exactly the reverse: they spend most of their money on material things that destroy money, and they put very little of their cash into **capital assets.**

HOME OWNERSHIP

A house is often the primary, if not only, piece of **capital** the average American family owns. Home ownership creates money for you, while you sleep, in several ways.

First, owning a home creates money for you because, as a rule, homes increase in value over time. Recently, this has not been as true as in the past, but depending on where you live, your home will decrease or increase in value as the years go by. In real estate parlance, "location, location, location" is the most important consideration when buying a home. A somewhat more expensive house in a "good" neighborhood will usually be a better investment than a cheaper house in a poorer neighborhood because a house in a good neighborhood usually increases in value with the years.

Whether your home is increasing in value or not, it is a means of forced savings. With every mortgage payment that you make, you create **equity**; that is, value in the house left over after you pay off your mortgage. You accumulate **equity** because part of each mortgage payment you make is **principal**, money that you pay directly to reduce your debt. If you were to sell your house, this **equity** or **principal** would be left over after you paid off your mortgage.

A third way homes create money results from tax breaks the federal government gives to homeowners. The interest on the mortgage payment is subtracted from your total income so that you do not pay taxes on that money. The interest portion of your payment is **non taxable** money. That is, while you may have to pay social security taxes and perhaps state income taxes on those dollars used to pay your mortgage, the federal government allows you to shelter the interest, to protect it from federal taxes.

Furthermore, as you sell each home you own, if you sell each house for more than you paid for it, making a profit on each house, you do not have to pay taxes on these **capital gains** until you sell your last house. You can simply use the profit or **capital gain** from one house to help you purchase a more expensive house. This kind of rollover of capital from one asset to another creates **tax-deferred dollars.** If you wait until after age 55 to sell your last house, you may never have to pay any taxes on the profits you have made through the sales of your homes.

Another way that home ownership helps you create capital is that a home equity loan provides a relatively cheap form of credit. By paying for some items with this cheaper credit, you can save money.

Also, the interest on home equity loans is often tax deductible on your federal income tax return, while the interest you pay on your credit cards and charge accounts is not deductible.

Homes also create money for owners through **leverage. Leverage** is the amount of debt you carry relative to your investment. For the purposes of this discussion, when home prices are going up, you make more money if you are **highly leveraged** or carrying quite a bit of debt on your home. It works this way.

You have bought a house for which you paid $100,000, and you have no mortgage on that house. The house goes up in value $5,000 during one year. You have earned 5% on your investment of $100,000.

Now, let's say you bought a $100,000 house but you only actually paid $20,000 down. The remaining $80,000 is a debt, a mortgage. Your house goes up $5,000 in value during the year. You have actually earned 25% rate of return: you earned $5,000 on the money you invested in that house, the original $20,000 down payment. In effect, you are using the bank's loan to you to make money for yourself. The total house increased in value by $5,000, but that increase in value can be percentaged against what you put into the house, which was only $20,000.

Leverage works to your advantage only when the price of real estate is increasing. However, the principle is important: wherever possible it is a good idea to use other people's money to make money for yourself, but you've got to watch those interest rate spreads, as discussed in the previous chapter. Using bank debt for this purpose is a legitimate use of debt, but must be used with caution. Sooner or later, all debt must be paid off. People get into trouble when they borrow too much money, become too highly **leveraged**, and their assets decline in value instead of increase in value. This leads to bankruptcy.

Now, contrast these advantages of home ownership with living in an apartment. None of your rent payment creates equity. All of your rent payment is money lost. All you have received for it is a roof over your head. You receive no forced savings because none of your payment goes toward **principal or building equity.** You receive no tax break from the federal government. You do not have an asset that is increasing in value to you that you can sell at some later date.

A basic principle about spending money wisely is WHEN YOU SPEND YOUR MONEY, TRY TO GET IT TO WORK DOUBLE FOR YOU. GET IT TO PURCHASE AT LEAST TWO THINGS AT ONCE FOR EACH DOLLAR SPENT.

For example, owning a home uses your dollar in many ways:

1. It provides you with shelter, and
2. It provides forced savings through repayment of **principal**, and
3. It gives you some **tax sheltered money** because of federal income tax deductions on the mortgage interest and the property taxes you pay, and
4. If you live in the right area, your home is increasing in value, and
5. It can provide a cheap source of credit through a home equity loan, and
6. It is increasing in value, it gives you a larger percentage **capital gain** because of **leverage,** and
7. Your home purchases can create **tax-deferred capital gains**.
8. By borrowing money for your mortgage, rather than paying off that mortgage if interest rates on it are low, you can play **interest rate spreads** to make more money for yourself.

For example, I have a home equity loan on my house that is averaging 7% interest. I used the money to create more **capital:** I added a sunroom and a garage. Instead of paying off that home equity loan all at once, I make my monthly payments, and keep money invested in mutual funds and other investments which are paying me between 10% and 15% rate of return. By not paying off my mortgage, I am actually earning money at a rate between 3% and 8% per year.

Thus, home ownership makes each dollar of your mortgage payment work in at least five or six different ways. Renting does none of these things. Each dollar of rent only pays for the rent.

A note on home equity loans--unless the money from home equity loans is used for **investments**, that is, used to purchase more capital (another home, home improvements, or more education for yourself), I do not recommend them. If they are used for more consumption, they will undermine the value of owning your home. Yes, you get a tax break on the interest payments, but you are not accumulating equity in your home, and your forced savings ceases. If you have a truly serious emergency--an automobile accident, severe personal injury--available equity in your home to borrow against to tide you through this emergency can mean the difference between financial ruin and financial security. You should not fritter this money-producing asset away on senseless consumption or transitory products or services.

CARS

Let's look at another asset that Americans spend money on: their cars. Americans now spend as much money on their cars as people used to spend on homes. Unless you own a classic car, which after twenty years may have increased in value, your automobile does two things: it provides you with transportation and it drains money out of your pocket, *and it drains this money out of your pocket in floods.* Unfortunately, for most people, besides basic transportation, cars also provide status and prestige and "kicks", but cars are a very expensive form of entertainment and "kicks."

Cars are considered an asset when you apply for loans because they are usually the next most valuable thing, after a home, that people own. However, I do not consider cars an asset. To my mind they are a colossal **liability**.

Get out your calculator and let's do some arithmetic.

CALCULATION:

Let's say you have spent $20,000 on your car. Assume that you will own that car for five years. Assume that you spend about $800 a year on automobile insurance, that you spend about $20 a week on gas, that you spend about $300 a year on oil changes, tune ups and minor repairs. These are bare minimum figures. What is the cost of your car for a year?

Car price averaged over 5 years ($20,000 divided by 5 years)	$4,000/year
Insurance	800
Gas ($20 x 52 weeks)	1,040
Repairs, maintenance	300

TOTAL CAR COST FOR ONE YEAR $6,140

Divide that $6,140 by 365 days and you learn that your car costs you $16.82 per day! This comes to $117.75 per week or $471.10 per month, not counting interest on time payments. If you buy your car on time payments, you pay additional interest per day, which will make your daily costs higher.

For example, recent advertisements in my local newspaper show the following:

CALCULATION:

1993 Prizm, cash price $9999, cost if bought over 60 months on payments: $11,992.80. Buying the car on credit adds nearly $2,000 to the cost of the car, or a 20% increase in the total cost to you. Dividing $2,000 in interest payments by 5 years means you pay $400 a year interest, which adds about another one dollar a day to the expenses of running your car.

Another ad shows a 1992 Chevrolet full size 4 x 4 truck for $11,799 cash price and $14,354 if paid over 60 months at $239.44 per month. That's a price increase of $2,555 for that truck if paid for on time payments, or $511 a year or $1.40 a day.

Figuring the cost of cars is difficult because you should count in the **depreciation** of the automobile, that is, the amount of value lost each year due to wear and tear on the automobile. Yes, you may have some resale value at the end of five years, but it will never equal what you originally paid for it.

Therefore, another way of estimating the cost of your automobile is to use the Internal Revenue Service's mileage and depreciation allowance. This figure is provided every year, and is used by businessmen who drive their cars for business purposes. Rather than keeping a log of every car expense incurred, a person can use the IRS mileage allowance on their tax returns to estimate the cost of owning and driving their cars per year. Recently the IRS upgraded their mileage rate to 29 cents a mile. Thus, if you drive your car 10,000 miles a year, you can estimate your expenses at $2,900 per year, or $7.95 a day.

Whichever way you figure it:

YOUR LARGEST CONTROLLABLE COST IS YOUR AUTOMOBILE.

Poor people often own expensive cars. I once had a welfare mother working for me. She told me that during the six years from the time when she got her driver's license until age 23 she had owned eight cars.

In August 1992, *Money* magazine published an article on Ross Perot and how he spends his money. Perot owned several cars, as shown below:

1. 1985 Oldsmobile
2. 1984 Chevrolet in Dallas
3. 1984 Chevrolet at his Vail home
4. Two 1985 Chevrolets at his home in Dallas
5. A 1989 Volvo
6. His wife owned a 1985 Jaguar sedan
7. The family owned another 1989 Jaguar, which probably belonged to the son, Ross Jr.

Notice the age of these cars and the makes. Six of these cars are practical, no nonsense means of transportation. Nothing very fancy here, and nothing very new. If anyone could afford expensive, high status cars, Ross Perot could, but he chooses to spend his money in other ways.

I am fifty-seven years old and have owned only five cars in my entire lifetime. Three of those cars were used when I bought them.

Cars are not assets. They are **liabilities** or things that drain your money. They are probably the most expensive waste of money you can ever experience except for paying credit card interest.

OTHER ASSETS THAT CREATE WEALTH

Besides owning a home, what assets do you have that can make money for you, or at least will not pour money away like water onto sand?

As discussed under the chapter on jobs, education is an asset. The more education you have, the more potential you have for increasing your earning power and for accumulating more money. As a rule, a highly educated person earns more per hour than a person who does not have much education. There are exceptions. We all know of college graduates who earn little and poorly educated people who have become millionaires. Nonetheless, for most people the key to a better economic future is more education.

I do not necessarily mean "college" education. I mean any classes that you take, at the local adult school, at the local community college, for credit or not, which hone your skills to enable you to become more effective in this world. Right now, any classes that you take to learn about computers will provide true value.

Your health is an asset. Good health is vital to maintaining your earning power and to increasing your enjoyment of life. Good health enables you to continue to work hard until you have enough money saved up to invest and begin producing money without your having to work. Undermining your health through poor eating habits, not getting enough sleep, smoking and other substance abuse is, among other things, a *foolish financial decision.* When reading the stories of successful people who started out life poor and ended it rich, you will often find that they worked two or three jobs at a time. It takes good health to do this.

I bootstrapped myself up by working two jobs at a time, actually three. I worked at a full time job in a corporation; I worked as a housewife doing all the things I've mentioned above, and during those hours when we did not work at our jobs, my husband and bought old houses, remodeled them, and re-sold them. This extra work enabled us to build up our **capital investments**, so that when we ultimately divorced, we each had enough money to own our homes--a rare occurrence for a divorcing couple.

Any available cash is an asset that can be used to make more money. This includes cash in savings accounts and checking accounts that is not earmarked for specific bills or purchases.

Your credit rating is an asset. Without a good credit rating, you cannot borrow money when you need it, and often borrowing money can save you money.

Nearly everything else that you spend your money on is a loss of capital: *All consumer goods take money away from capital accumulation.* Furniture, cigarettes, cars, clothing, cosmetics, liquor, entertainment, all of these items take money away from **capital accumulation.** Yes, many of these consumer goods are necessities. We must spend money on them, but to spend excess money on them in the name of "status" and "prestige" is to throw money down the drain. These are the foolish items on which people waste their money.

Therefore, when you buy things, ask yourself these questions.

1) Does this item put money into my pocket or take money out of my pocket, either now or in the long-term?
2) If I must purchase this item, and it does drain money out of my pocket, is it draining it quickly or slowly?
3) Can I use this item to make more money to compensate for its purchase?

My mother and I used to sit up until the wee small hours of the mornings talking about "home economics." She always said that, "The man brings the money in the front door, and the woman throws it out the back door with the dish water." She always believed it was not how much money you earned that counted, but how you spent what you have, and her life was a testimony to the success of that approach to money handling.

My father started his married life earning $18 a week. My mother said it took them five years to pay the doctor who attended my birth. My mother really scratched around to obtain that first $2,000 of capital so that they could build and own their first house. Then she saved and saved so that they *never* bought a car on time payments. And she *never* paid charge card interest. When her father died, he left her just about $2,000 worth of stock in the Great Western Sugar Company. Mom parlayed that small amount of money into investments in real estate rental properties, stocks, and ultimate financial security for herself and my father. She never worked at a job outside the home, but she made every moment inside that house count. She sewed. She cooked. She did home repairs better than my father. And she educated herself about investments by listening to financial programs on the radio and TV and by reading *The Wall Street Journal* every day.

The world has changed since then, but the financial principles remain the same. In the chapters below, I will discuss in greater detail the differences between spending your money wisely and spending it stupidly. The important thing to know is that there is a difference. Just as all dollars are not equal, not all types of spending are equal.

CHAPTER SIX: HIDDEN COSTS AND DEPRECIATION

Thus far, we have discussed down shifting your spending from buying consumer goods to buying **capital assets** whenever possible. However, you still must buy consumer goods and products. In the past you've been taught to "shop around", get the best price before buying any product, but calculating the true costs of products or services is not easy because there are **hidden costs and depreciation.**

Depreciation is a decrease or loss in value because of wear, age, or other causes. As soon as you buy any new product, as soon as you take it out of the store, it depreciates. You cannot turn around and sell it for what you paid for it. Anyone who has sold things at a garage sale or a yard sale knows this truth.

When managing your money, try to minimize the effects of depreciation. The easiest and most effective way to do this is to buy as many things *used* as possible. Let other people suffer the effects of depreciation. You reap the benefits.

Baby clothes for example. I have friends who never buy new baby clothes. Women in the neighborhood get together and run a sale every year of used baby clothes, basically swapping among themselves as their children age or as new babies arrive. Certainly the babies themselves do not care what they wear as long as they are clean and comfortable.

Luxury items depreciate faster and more severely than utilitarian objects. China dishes provide a case in point. I bought a set of fine china for $1100 several years ago. The set included place-settings for twelve people with serving dishes and elegant gilt trimmed soup bowls. The price retail, on sale, came to $91.66 cents for each place setting. I tried to sell my china recently. I could not get anyone to offer me $50 a place setting. This china is in mint condition--not a crack, not a chip to be seen, barely used.

Similarly with crystal goblets. I have a set of crystal which I priced at retail at $129 a stem over a year ago. This price did not include 6% sales tax. I was unable to sell this crystal for $50 a stem at my garage sale. I finally sold some of it for $25 a stem. Again, the crystal was in absolutely perfect condition.

Learn from my experience. Never pay retail or sale prices for new crystal or china. Read the ads in your local newspapers. People who are getting divorced, who are moving, who need cash, sell valuable items at a fraction of what they would cost you new. Haunt garage sales and yard sales. Here you save *real* money.

The American economy produces a surfeit of *things*. Most people have too much stuff. People live in their own individual homes. Parents live separately from their children. When the parents die, all their furniture and belongings must be sold off since, as a rule, the children already have completely furnished homes. These sales provide a buying opportunity for you.

People in this society move around constantly. Every time a household moves, they will jettison much of their "stuff" at a garage sale because it is usually more economical to sell it and buy new things at the other end of the move rather than pay the moving charges to ship things to the new home.

Jewelry is another product that depreciates immediately after you buy it. Regardless of its so-called appraised value, you will never be able to sell it for what you paid for it unless you keep it until it is antique. I buy my jewelry at flea markets where dealers who have purchased "estate" jewelry are re-selling it again. Yes, this is risky business, but no more risky than paying full price for jewelry at a department store or jewelry store, taking it home, and having it lose half its value immediately.

Buy antique furniture if you can, rather than furniture from a department store or furniture store. You may not make a profit if you wish to re-sell your antiques, but you can usually get back what you paid for them, sometimes even more. If you buy the usual store furniture, you will never get any money out of it. Your only recourse is to use it until it has fallen apart.

I recently sold a wall unit, cherry traditional, for which I paid over $2,000. I used it for six years. When I priced the same wall unit this year, the retail cost, *on sale*, was nearly $3,500. I sold mine for $500, and it was in nearly perfect condition.

Let's calculate the real cost of that wall unit:

$2,000 divided by 6 years = $120 a year for the cherry wall unit.

It is true, I would never have sold the wall unit except that I moved into a smaller house. It was a piece of furniture that I could have kept for my entire lifetime. It would never have worn out or gone out of style. Sometimes these things happen. Still, it was an expensive piece of furniture when the cost is calculated against the number of years I used it. If you will force yourself to wait, to watch the garage sale ads in your local newspaper, you will find excellent bargains for a fraction of the cost of what you would pay for the same things in a store.

Now, to **hidden costs**. One of the most common hidden costs is *upkeep*. When you buy a suit or coat that needs to be dry cleaned, you pay the initial price and then the cleaning bills. You can pay for a garment several times over in cleaning bills alone. I no longer buy any garment that I cannot wash.

The hidden cost of keeping things clean can clean out your wallet. For example, one serious decorating trap is "white." Look at the pictures in the decorating magazines. How many times do you see living room rugs that are "white," couches and chairs that are "white," bedroom accessories that are "white." I agree that white is gorgeous, but it is very expensive to keep clean. One immediate way to save money is never to buy white covered furniture and rugs for interior decoration.

I had a friend who redecorated her living room. The centerpiece of the room was a huge white couch. Within days, the arms of the sofa were blackened because her husband read *The New York Times* while sitting on the sofa, and the ink from the newspaper bled onto his hands and from there onto the sofa.

Another serious hidden cost occurs in foods. When you buy so-called fast foods or prepared foods, you pay the cost of the food and over time, you may pay additional medical bills resulting from poor nutrition. This may sound far fetched, but it is true. Your body is like a computer: garbage in, garbage out. Almost daily one can read articles in newspapers and magazines about the effects of poor nutrition on such diseases as cancer, heart disease and osteoporosis. Every time you drink a can of carbonated soda, the phosphates in the soda drain calcium out of your system, which can lead to fragile bones as you age. As discussed earlier, you also pay for packaging, for marketing, and for advertising when you buy convenience foods. These are the hidden costs of this type of food.

I do not regard economizing on food as a true economy. I have always bought the highest quality foods in terms of freshness and variety, and I don't comparison shop. Good health is priceless. Quality food provides the best insurance against poor health. Skipping meals may save you money in the short run, but in the long run your health will suffer.

My first husband always insisted that to save money I should "cut the food budget." I did cut it in the ways I have discussed above. I never bought convenience foods, and I always bought the cheapest cuts of meat to make stews or soups instead of having steaks or chops. But we always ate butter, eggs, fresh fruits and vegetables.

Hidden costs in foods are difficult to find because of the labeling. Peanut butter for example. Most commercial peanut butter contains shortening. Shortening is cheap and nutritionally hazardous because it is pure homogenized fat. Price out a can of shortening. When you pay for shortening in peanut butter, it becomes expensive. Manufacturers put shortening in peanut butter to make it smooth and to keep the natural oils in the peanuts from separating out. When you buy pure peanut butter, you've got to spend some time stirring it up so the oil mixes in properly. Then you've got to keep it refrigerated after you open it. This seems like a small price to pay for pure, nutritious food instead of a food saturated with shortening.

This example of peanut butter is another argument for cooking your foods from scratch. At least that way you know what's in your food, and you are paying money for true value. When you buy potatoes that are still potatoes, carrots that are still carrots, and oranges that are still oranges, you are paying for real food, not over processed substitutes.

Another example of hidden food costs occurs when ordinary ingredients are combined into a different form, labeled as something "fancy", dressed in an elaborate package, and then sold as something new. One popular example of this process is the new European coffees. They come in small cans and cost a great deal of money compared to ordinary coffee. When you read the label, you will find that they contain nothing you probably don't already have at home: instant coffee, some soy based dried creamers, flavorings, a thickening agent.

Smoking and drinking provide the most obvious examples of severe hidden costs: the initial costs of the cigarettes and the liquor plus the subsequent deterioration of health that results. Modern health professionals believe that smoking is the most serious source of preventable health problems in the population. Smoking leads to birth defects, cancers, heart disease, and lung diseases--all of them preventable if one does not smoke. These are very high costs associated with smoking, in addition to the very high costs of buying the cigarettes themselves. If you are serious about saving money, stop smoking!

Cars entail severe hidden and not so hidden costs. One of the most common hidden costs is mileage. People drive their cars randomly without counting the cost of using that car. The costs include not only gas, which is obvious, but wear and tear on the tires and the engine parts. As discussed earlier The Internal Revenue Service allows businesses to deduct 29 cents per mile for wear and tear and general depreciation of an automobile used for business purposes.

You should regard your personal automobile the same way. When you make that extra trip to the supermarket to get a carton of milk or to pick up a newspaper, count in the costs of using your car at 29 cents per mile. For example, you decide to take a trip to the local deli to pick up a newspaper. The deli is a half mile away, one mile round trip. The newspaper costs $1.00 -- it's Sunday. If you drive to the deli, the cost of that newspaper is:

Newspaper = $1.00
Plus mileage 1 mile at 29 cents
Total cost of newspaper $1.29.

That's the real cost of the newspaper. Multiply this by the dozens of little trips that people routinely make in their cars. They would be better off, both economically and in terms of their health, to buy a bicycle and use it to make any trips under two miles. With the recent increase in the gasoline tax, the cost of driving has gone higher.

I live 40 miles from the nearest town. It's an 80 mile round trip to do my grocery shopping. Because of this, I make out a long list of errands before I leave for town. I try to do everything possible in one weekly trip. So, I go to the hardware store, the bank, the post office, the feed store to buy bird seed, the grocery store, the bookstore, the Wal-Mart, the liquor store for a bottle of wine, and at the very last, I fill up my car gas tank, fill up the 2 1/2 gallon cans for my snowmobile, and return home. As a result of my cost consciousness, I am putting only about 5,000 miles a year on my car instead of 15,000 that I used to That extra 10,000 miles a year occurred mainly from making several short trips instead of one big weekly trip to the stores. Driving 10,000 fewer miles at a rough cost of 29 cents a mile saves me $2900 a year in automobile costs.

Car pooling avoids some of these costs. My neighbor bought a mini-van. One of the hidden costs of buying the mini-van was that all her neighbors decided since she had the largest car, she could pick up all of *their* kids after the soccer games and basketball games. She did not want to offend her neighbors, but finally she had to firmly say no to them or else arrange car pooling where everyone shared the costs of picking up the kids. If she cuts out one eight mile trip per week through car pooling she saves:

CALCULATION: 8 x 29 cents = $2.32 plus about an hour of her time at $10 an hour = a total savings of $12.32

Major hidden costs appear when you buy a new or a luxury car. First, your insurance rates increase dramatically because you pay for collision and theft insurance as well as liability. Secondly, your replacement parts for the new car are much more expensive. Your tires may be of a larger size on the new car. Your hub caps and spoked wheels are very expensive. Your repair bills may become more expensive because these newer cars are more difficult to repair. These are all reasons for driving your old clunker until it falls apart.

I have friends who recently bought a new pick-up truck. They shopped and shopped to find the best "deal." They do need a pick-up truck occasionally because they are avid gardeners, and they buy manure and top soil for their garden. They also do many house repairs, so they need a truck occasionally to bring home sheets of plywood. However, the number of days they really *need* a pick-up truck is probably no more than ten a year.

I offered to sell them my old Subaru station wagon for $800. It was in very good condition, with new tires and about 90,000 miles on it. I had changed the oil every 3,000 miles, and kept the interior pretty clean, despite the hard use I gave it hauling my own pieces of lumber and plywood. They declined. If they had bought the Subaru, they could have easily afforded to rent a truck whenever they needed one. The rental fees could have been more than paid for by what they would have saved in finance charges, insurance and depreciation on the new pick-up truck they bought instead of the old Subaru station wagon.

These people are not wealthy. They have two young children that they do not plan to send to college unless the kids can earn their own way through scholarships. The amount of money they are spending on a pickup truck would send one of those children to college for about two years.

<u>CALCULATION:</u> If they took that money they spent on the new truck, let's say $10,000 to make things easy, and invested it at 10% compounded, at the end of 10 years they would have $108,000 -- enough to send both children to college and then some.

When I see families spending money on new cars instead of saving for their children's college educations, it makes me mad! The whole society suffers, but the children will suffer the most. In the coming future, children must have advanced education in order to obtain highly technical jobs--the only kinds of jobs this economy is creating. The alternative is to spend one's life in low paying service jobs--waitresses, typists, clerks in stores. The higher paying, union, blue collar manufacturing jobs are disappearing out of our economy.

My former business partner drives his cars into the ground, until they are past the point of being junk. When he wants to take a vacation trip, he rents a new car just for that trip. The money he saves on depreciation, higher insurance rates, and no finance charges by driving his cars until they drop more than pays for those few times when he rents a car.

Unfortunately, when people think of buying a car, they only look at the costs of purchasing the car but the costs of upkeep are more significant when multiplied over the life of the car. One of the most important costs is your gas mileage. If you buy a car that averages 18 miles per gallon of gas, and you drive 15,000 miles a year, your gasoline costs at $1.15 a gallon will be:

> <u>CALCULATION:</u> 15,000 miles divided by 18 mpg = 833.33 gallons of gas per year x $1.15 = $958.32 dollars for gasoline.
>
> Compare this with a car that averages 25 miles per gallon of gasoline:
>
> 15,000 miles divided by 25 = 600 gallons x $1.10 = $690 dollars for gasoline, or a savings of $268.32 per year.

When buying a house or renting an apartment, look for hidden costs. Windows for example. If you live where there are cold winters, the more and the bigger your windows, the higher your heating costs. Is there a cathedral ceiling in your new house? That higher ceiling will cost you more in heating bills. Is that house or apartment located near or far from shopping? The farther away from shopping, the more you will spend on gasoline. That is a hidden *housing* cost.

Of course, the same holds true for distance from your job. The farther from your job you live, the higher your transportation costs. Maybe your mortgage or rent is lower, but in fact, your housing may not be cheaper because of the higher transportation costs. This is often a trade off to consider when renting or buying a house.

As discussed earlier, there are hidden costs associated with your job. It may be more economical for you to take a job at a lower salary where you can dress casually everyday, rather than taking a higher paying job where you must be perfectly and expensively dressed, where you must have your hair done frequently.

As a rule, when I buy appliances, I try to buy those that have the fewest automatic features, believing that the more complicated they are, the more likely they are to break down. I bought a two head VCR because the sales clerk told me that a four head VCR often entails more frequent and more expensive repairs. I am not sophisticated enough to see the additional picture clarity provided by four heads.

Repairs and upkeep are major hidden costs. Whenever you buy anything, do not look simply at the sticker price, but look down the road at the upkeep and the repair costs. And when you spend money, try to avoid depreciation; buy USED.

CHAPTER SEVEN: SHOPPING FOR VALUE

The only "home economics" most women have been taught is to comparison shop. If this is what you've been taught, you have probably discovered that no matter how hard you try, you cannot get ahead financially by comparison shopping.

I believe most comparison shopping is a complete waste of time. I do urge you to comparison shop for interest rate plays among your credit card charges, your bank fees, and other interest rates. Comparison shopping on large ticket items--mainly cars and houses--is worth your time and energy. However, with those exceptions, I have tried to demonstrate that you can usually save more money by doing it yourself, at home, than you can by traditional comparison shopping based solely on ticket price, especially comparison shopping for food, clothing and home furnishings..

Comparison shopping deals almost totally with price differences, but when you shop on the basis of price, you run into the problem of determining quality, and this is not always easy. For example, I recently bought a queen sized quilted bed pad at a discount bed and bath store. When I got it home and unpackaged it, I found that the bed pad was too small by many inches. Rather than go through the hassle and expense of returning it, (a **time versus money calculation** of the hour or so driving time, the gasoline mileage and wear on my car to return something and replace it with something that might be just as unsatisfactory and more costly), I pieced it out using remnants from the old bed pad and sewed it back together. It doesn't look so great, but I'm the only one who will notice it.

I had no way of discovering the quality of this "cheap" bed pad until I got home and unwrapped it. It was described as a "queen sized" bed pad, but there were no dimensions given on the package, so I could not really check it out. It was closer to a double bed size than a queen.

Determining quality of towels, sheets, and much clothing is similarly difficult. You buy cheaper sheets and find they have no hems or that they are too short to tuck underneath your mattress. You buy towels that do not absorb moisture. You stand there in the bathroom, rubbing yourself raw, but all you do is smear moisture around on your skin until it evaporates. You buy clothing that is too short, has no hems, or the buttons unravel and fall off at the first opportunity. What you save in price you often lose in quality.

Basically, I have tried to encourage you to hang onto your money by not buying things except when absolutely necessary. Nonetheless, there are times, like virtually every day, when one must buy things in the open market of the American economy. If one doesn't comparison shop, how does one know that she or he is getting good deals on purchased items?

No matter how clever a shopper you are, the merchandisers are cleverer. I worked in market research for 30 years; I know what "marketing" means. It means designing packaging, advertising, and displays in ways to manipulate the consumer to buy more things, preferably at higher prices, than the consumer needs. I read *The Wall Street Journal.* Periodically that newspaper runs articles on merchandising and advertising ploys: how to arrange shelves and products to entice the consumer. How to advertise more effectively to motivate consumers to buy, buy, buy whether they need it or not. At one level, I cannot criticize this business, because it keeps the American economy moving along, but marketing scams can bankrupt an unwary consumer.

Where do you begin? I believe you should start with two principles:

1) Identify one or two stores, or a specific mail order catalogue company, and buy everything from them.

2) When you've identified a quality store or catalogue company, then buy what you love.

When I catalogue shop, I comparison shop enough to know when one company's prices are *reasonable,* and I have bought enough from them to know I can depend upon the quality of what I purchase. Notice I say their prices are *reasonable*, not the lowest prices around, but good prices for good quality.

Buy what you love! How many times have you bought a great "bargain" -- a pair of shoes or a hat or a handbag that was a bit ugly, not quite what you liked but "so cheap!" Then, you take it home, put it in your closet and never wear it again. This is not a bargain. Who has not done this?

My sister-in-law shops endlessly, especially for furniture. She asks my advice, and all I can say is, "Buy what you love. If you love it, you will use it." But she is obsessed with price, with buying things cheaply (despite the fact that she admitted she keeps a running balance on her charge card). She and her husband do not earn a great deal of money, and she feels guilty if she doesn't buy things "on sale." She shops and shops, wandering from store to store, like some ghost pining over this and that item that she cannot really afford. Finally, she buys something--a rug, a bedspread, a sofa-- that is "cheap". She takes it home and hates it because it is not lovely. To economize, she will buy secondhand furniture or take furniture for free even when it is ugly.

I have urged you to buy secondhand furniture to save money, but I have always thought of this as a stopgap measure until you can afford to buy what you love. In this instance, if my sister-in-law would pay off the running balance on her charge card, stuff the monthly payments she usually makes into a cookie jar, she could eventually replace the secondhand furniture with pieces she loves. But she does not do this. So she hates it when she brings such stuff home. Then she doesn't love her home. She casts her eyes about, and everywhere she sees disappointment. She lives in that house everyday. It depresses her. She should love everything in it. That's what a home should be: a haven, a place of love and beauty.

This chapter is about "value." Ugliness is a poor value. To live in ugliness more than you have to destroys your morale. Beauty is important, and you should not feel guilty for desiring beauty in your surroundings.

When I was very poor, I had no furniture to speak of: a mattress on the floor for a sofa, an easy chair bought at the Salvation Army Store, a few other very old chairs, and homemade curtains at some of the windows. I was lucky that my mother had given me a few beautiful things: a pair of Victorian brass candlesticks, a pewter chocolate pot. Wherever I moved, into the most dingy houses and apartments, I took my "pewter pots" with me. As soon as I had moved in, I arranged these things on some windowsill or table to make a little patch of beauty in an otherwise ugly home environment. I have bought a few beautiful dishes or tea pots in antique stores to create a few islands of beauty in my home until I could afford to buy more: a cut glass bowl filled with fruit on the kitchen table, a lace dresser scarf, a few old vases for my flowers, a silver plated sugar bowl for my dining table.

If you have a choice between a piece of furniture that is mediocre or ugly but cheap, don't buy it unless you know it is absolutely temporary. As a rule, I recommend that you use cinder blocks and boards until you can save enough money to buy a piece of furniture that you love. When your furniture is obviously junk, you can laugh about it. It costs you nothing. Buy at the Good Will or Salvation Army if you need a chair, or swipe chairs sitting out at the curb for trash collection. I have done this until I can save the money to buy what I really want. Your friends won't think any the less of you. Some of my happiest parties occurred around a plank set on two cinder blocks, where we all sat on the floor and used the plank for our table. It's very democratic and intimate and fun.

When figuring the cost of any purchase, you must think of more than the price you pay for it. You must also divide that price, at least mentally, by the number of times you will use that product. Thus, if you pay $200 for a suit that you love, and you wear it once every week for 52 weeks, it costs you $3.84 each time you wear it the first year. On the other hand if you pay $200 for a fancy party dress that you wear twice, it costs you $100 each time you wear it for the first year. Which is the greater value? The dress that you wear twice or the suit that you wear constantly?

When you shop, think in terms of **value**, not simply price. I think the biggest error that American shoppers make is to concentrate on price rather than value. But what is **value?**

A product has the following kinds of value:

1. It can be worth money when you re-sell it, preferably worth more money than when you purchased it. This is its **appreciation** value.

2. A product can have **utility** value. It is useful to you. You will use it again and again. I have a rolling pin, some mixing bowls and cooking pots that I bought when I was 21 years old.

3. A product can have **pleasure** value. It makes you feel good, it gives you delight, enhances your overall life every time you use it. A good down comforter can give you this pleasure, or a small Oriental rug, or a porcelain toothbrush holder in the bathroom.

4. A product can provide **status or image** value. By using this product you will appear to be some sort of superior person: more beautiful, more sexually attractive, smarter, more sophisticated. Cars usually fall into this category, but the house you buy, the neighborhood in which you live, whether you wear polyester blouses or silk blouses, all provide status or image value.

5. A product can have **longevity** value. That is, it can last for years and years. Antiques have this kind of value. They are timeless. Tools can have this kind of value. A pair of pliers never wears out if they are of good quality. I have leather boots that I've had for years and continue to wear.

When shopping, try to get as many of the values listed above for each dollar you spend. For example, twenty years ago I bought an antique walnut Pennsylvania slant top desk. I paid $2,000 for it. At the time, (and at this time for that matter), this purchase seemed like an outright extravagance, but I bought the desk because I loved it. I also bought it because I could use it. It had **utility.** It could be used as a desk. It has four big drawers, plus the pull down desk top and many cubbyholes to store papers in. It is also a beautiful piece of furniture, one that I have always kept in my living room, and thus, this desk offers **pleasure** value for me. Every time I look at it, it warms my heart with the beautiful tone of the wood, its gracefully shaped ogee feet, its stolid permanence.

This desk has **status** value. I lived near Princeton, a hotbed of antique collectors and dealers. Many of my friends entirely furnished their homes with antiques. I wanted to emulate them, to be one of them, so I bought antiques.

This desk has **longevity value.** I've had it twenty years. Despite the entreaties of antiques dealers, I did not sell it when I moved to the mountains of Colorado. The Pennsylvania desk sits, glowing beautifully, in the sunlight in the corner of my new house. When I moved here, as soon as that desk was placed in its corner of the living room, this house became a home for me. The desk is family. I hope to have it until the day I die. Every time I look at it, it comforts me, reassures me. I think of the loving hands that built it over two hundred years ago, and I love it and cherish it as part of that tradition.

At the time, that $2,000 seemed sheer folly, but that desk has turned out to be one of the best, most economical purchases I have ever made. Compare it with the cherry wall unit I described earlier, which I was able to sell for only a fraction of what I paid for it. The antiques dealers who saw the desk recently offered me $4,000 for it. Thus, it had **appreciation** value as well as all the other values I have listed above.

Obviously, everybody reading this book cannot rush out to buy a Pennsylvania slant top desk, or any other antiques for that matter. I use the desk as an example of getting five different uses out of each dollar I spent. When you buy, try to do the same thing.

The United States is a "mature" economy. That means that most people have the essentials of comfort. A vast majority of households have washing machines, televisions, telephones, and most have at least one car if not two. Once basic needs have been satisfied, how do manufacturers continue to sell things? They do it by shifting from **utility** value in their advertisements and marketing to **status** values. They create discontent in you with what you have and who you are, and you go out and buy new things to satisfy that discontent.

Notice the automobile advertisements. Rarely do they emphasize utility. The closest they come now is to emphasize "safety", which is a utility value, but few ads push safety. They push glamour, performance, sophistication, status. Some cars advertise low price too.

Still, are glamour, sophistication, status, and sex appeal values that you can afford? Most people cannot. You need transportation, and you need the cheapest, most economical transportation you can get. When you buy an automobile, comparison shop for price by all means, but the greater savings will be achieved by buying a car that is strictly utilitarian with high gas mileage rather than a car that is glamorous or fast, or sexy, and you will save more money if you manage to buy a quality used car.

Earlier, I urged you to buy what you love, but obviously, when it comes to cars, I put a big caution on that principle. If what you love is a BMW or a new Lexus and what you need is a Dodge, then you should go for the Dodge. The savings you will achieve are so immense, that you could use the money you save to take a safari to Africa at some future date, or send one of your children to college if you take the money saved and invest it prudently. Cars are one place where you should place **utility before love.**

From the discussion above, you can see that buying **value** is a very personal act. One person's value is another person's idiocy. I am simply urging you to become conscious of what is motivating your purchases and how that affects you economically over the short term and the long term. Buy what you love, but only if it also has **longevity or appreciation value,** or if it is reasonably priced.

I have a friend who is a union electrician. He shops for his work shirts at a used clothing store. He says, "Why should I pay $15 for a work shirt that I'm going to get all greasy and torn up when I can buy one for $1.50 used?" Why indeed? This man understands the difference between paying for utility and paying for status. He buys old American cars. I don't believe he has ever bought a new car in his life. Yet he has his own airplane. The guys at his job envy him. They think he's rich. The plane gives him great pleasure and delight. He says, "They think that plane costs a lot of money, but I didn't pay any more for it than those guys pay for a car."

This man is actively planning an early retirement. He takes 4 - 5 weeks a year off for vacations. He hauls his little camper trailer down to a favorite spot in Florida and stays there, to fish and relax and enjoy himself in the sunshine. His little house is completely paid for and furnished with very old furniture. People tease him mercilessly about being cheap. Yet he doesn't owe a dime to anyone. He always has money available to do what he loves to do: to fly, to eat dinners out, to take long vacations. Status and prestige mean nothing to him. He looks for pleasure, utility, longevity *and* a good price.

I recently had to undergo an insurance physical exam. I began talking with the nurse who came to my house to give me the exam. She was a single parent with two children. She received no support money from her ex-husband. She was as cheerful, energetic and hard working as anyone I have ever met, but she had her economic values completely skewed, and these skewed values kept her very poor.

One of the biggest mistakes you can do, financially, is to "buy into the American Market Economy," the so-called American financial dream. This woman had done just that. Her purchases were entirely influenced by status, prestige, brand name values instead of utility, longevity, and appreciation.

As we talked, she bragged, in a nice way, that she never bought any of her clothes at KMart. That she never bought fake perfumes but only genuine designer fragrances. She spent "good money" on her clothing, her hair, her personal care products. By this she meant she always bought "name brand" products rather than house brands or cheap, unknown brands. Interspersed with these comments, she complained about the difficulties she faced raising her children, caring for them properly, that she was stuck in a dead end, low paying job and could barely meet her rent payments.

I questioned her further. It turned out that she only earned about $7.50 an hour as a nurse. However, she received no benefits, and more importantly, she was *not reimbursed for the use of her car* when she had to travel to people's homes to give the insurance physicals. She had driven up from Cherry Hill to near Princeton to take my physical exam, and she received *absolutely no compensation for the use of her car or her travel time.*

I sat with her, got out my calculator, and showed her that she had a net loss for her trip up to see me. She was being paid for only the time spent with me--not the two hours of travel time. The mileage to and from Cherry Hill is about 72 miles and at the IRS mileage allowance at that time, it had cost her $19.80 (27.5 cents x 72 miles) to drive the distance to my house.

Here's the arithmetic:

CALCULATION: Money earned at $7.50 per hour x two hours at my house = $15.00

Subtract Expenses	
Car: 72 mi x 27.5 cents)	$19.80
Two hours travel time not reimbursed	$15.00
Total costs to her of the trip:	$34.80

Subtract amount earned from costs leaves a LOSS of $19.80. It's actually worse than that, because she must pay income taxes and social security withholding on the $15 she earned. It had never entered her mind to calculate in the costs of her travel time and car use as expenses to subtract from her wages. She should never have agreed to drive that distance to my house. She'd have been better off economically to stay at home watching soaps on TV.

As she rambled on about her financial difficulties and her pride in paying "top dollar" for "brand names," I sat there in some despair. She was a wonderful person, but daily she made small decisions that were bankrupting her future and that of her children. She was talking to a person who earned in excess of $50,000 a year, had complete medical coverage, and absolutely no hesitation about shopping at

KMart. She was talking to a person who practically never wears perfume let alone pays $40 an ounce for it. She was talking to a person who used witch hazel as a facial astringent rather than paying $20 a pint for "brand name" facial astringents in the department and cosmetic stores. She was talking to a person who cut her own hair and wore blue jeans to work.

Does this struggling nurse really think that *anyone* in her circle of friends could possibly smell the difference between a real Chanel fragrance and an imitation or cheaper fragrance? Does she believe that anyone really *cares*? I felt very sorry for her, because she was obtaining her own sense of personal value from those phony, very expensive products she hung on her body: perfumes, clothing, handbags, make up.

Please do not think that I have not struggled with misplaced status issues. I too have wanted to be admired and respected by my friends, especially my friends who were wealthier than I. I have wanted to be stylish, beautiful, sexy, successful looking. Fortunately, I have learned that most status is absolutely hollow beyond a certain point. Yes, there is a basic threshold of "image" which is important. You've got to look clean, competent, and attractive in our society to get good jobs and nice apartments, to be treated with respect by doctors, lawyers, and other professional people, but there are places where you can draw a line and save lots of money.

Clothing, for example. When I worked as a professional market researcher and met with important clients in New York, Washington, D.C., and all points in between, I dressed to maintain an image of a smart, professional woman. Every year, I went to a specialty dress shop in Princeton where one sales lady had exquisite taste. She chose my clothes and accessories for me because I don't have very good taste when it comes to clothes. I bought one fine wool pantsuit in winter and one new lightweight pantsuit each summer. At the time, these suits ranged in price from $150 each to $300. They were brand name, beautifully tailored suits.

Now, let's examine these purchases more closely. First, they were pantsuits. I realize that not all women are comfortable in pantsuits, but I am tall and lean. For me they were ideal in terms of "looks." However, they performed several other **utility** functions. They were timeless. Hemlines on pantsuits don't change. Therefore, I did not have to buy a new coat each year to compensate for changing hemlines.

They were extremely comfortable during airplane and train travel. I could climb on and off little commuter airlines without having gusts of wind blow my skirts over my head. In winter, I could wear cotton socks and boots with them, which were warmer and kept my feet dry. I could run for trains and subways without falling or twisting my ankles because I could wear low healed shoes with these suits.

One thing further: I bought these suits in colors that could be accessorized with black, blue, or brown shoes and handbags. I bought leather shoes and handbags, some of which I still have. By limiting my colors, I did not have to completely re-accessorize my wardrobe each time I bought a new suit. This is an example of **hidden costs**, which I discussed earlier. Changing wardrobe colors and styles incurs hidden costs of completely changing your accessories.

Some of those suits I wore for ten years. They were beautiful, appropriate, and comfortable. True, they were not sexy. They were not particularly noticeable, but neither is men's clothing. Why do you think men wear the standard suit and tie, year after year? For all of the reasons I've listed above. Utility, comfort, and efficiency.

Fashion for women is just about the biggest rip-off in the American economy. The sooner you extricate yourself from that nonsense, the sooner you will be financially independent and able to do more important things with your life. Fashion is designed specifically to keep women buying and shopping, spending their money. It has nothing to do with real value, but only facade and image.

To repeat, I believe image is important. To be successful in the world, you must look successful. Quality clothing is part of that image, but fashion is not.

As for jewelry, I have always bought antique jewelry at flea markets. I love the pieces that I buy, and when I wear them on my pantsuits, they shine forth with originality and class. I can wear those pieces until the day I die, and my estate will be able to sell them for more than I paid for them. I have a few pieces of costume jewelry that are classics, chosen for me by the sales lady at the specialty dress shop. I shall wear them forever too. I have not bought a new piece of jewelry for years. I never get tired of what I have now because the pieces are beautiful, timeless, elegant. Also, up here in the mountains, who needs jewelry?

When shopping for clothing, buy for **utility and longevity,** as well as price, but be sure that you **love** what you buy so that you will wear it often. It's got to look good on you, or you will not be comfortable. Being comfortable inside your clothes leads to being comfortable inside your skin, and then you can approach the world with confidence and radiance.

Let's talk about value in food shopping. "Buy what you love" still holds. We eat every day. Why not make each meal a pleasure, a culinary joy, another piece of beauty in your life? A well known writer of cookbooks remarks, "Since we must eat to live, we might as well do it with both grace and gusto." (M.E.K. Fisher)

I love food. I cannot afford to eat out, but I can prepare luxurious meals at home for less money than I can eat fast food at a greasy restaurant.

Take prime rib roasts, for example. They now cost about $20 if they are large enough to feed four people. If you throw in some baked potatoes, toss a green salad and top it with your homemade salad dressings, uncork a bottle of American jug wine, some of which are excellent, you have created a tasty, luxurious meal for about $35 for 4 people. To buy a similar meal in a restaurant, including the tip, will easily cost you $80 or more.

Lobster seems like the epitome of an expensive meal, far beyond the reach of ordinary people. So it is if you eat it in a restaurant. But some of my pleasantest meals have been at-home dinners, kitchen dinners I call them, with steamed lobster, corn on the cob, fresh sliced tomatoes and cucumbers, and cold wine, a simple feast eaten by candlelight.

Each meal can be festive and joyous. Food is not only something to stuff in your gut, but it carries associations of hospitality, pleasure, happiness and sharing. Yes, I think cooking is one of the best ways to save money, but it is also one of the best ways to give yourself daily pleasure. I cannot recommend enough that when you shop for food, buy what you love (provided that it is also basically nutritious). A diet of ice cream is not recommended.

Every day, for breakfast, I treat myself to hot oat bran with pecans and raisins and brown sugar, a big mug of espresso cafe au alit, and a fresh soft boiled egg every other day. I slice fresh bananas and mix them with a variety of canned or fresh fruit. (I'm allergic to oranges). I take enough time to savor this delicious food. It brightens my day.

I have talked about the virtues of brown bagging your lunches. They don't have to be boring, tasteless affairs. Many offices now provide microwave ovens for their employees. When you cook meatloaf, or spaghetti, or broiled chicken, make enough for leftovers to take in your lunches. Heat them in the microwave.

Earlier, I mentioned trying to sell some expensive crystal and the problem of **depreciation.** I did not mention that I had purchased that Baccarat crystal for $10 a stem when I was a secretary. I was looking for status. I was also looking for beauty. I bought the crystal because it was beautiful, and would go with both a casual table setting and one more ornate. I don't quite know why I chose the Baccarat crystal, but I knew it was beautiful and of high quality. It was a quality, brand name purchase. It **appreciated** in value over the years. Not a great deal, but some. True, I can only sell it for $25 a stem, but that is still better than most brands of crystal you can buy. This crystal fulfilled the following values: **utility, status, pleasure, longevity and appreciation.** While I sold some of it when I moved, I have kept some of it. If nothing else, I can give it as a wedding present to one of my nieces, or I can continue to use it and enjoy it for the rest of my life.

Compare this with buying name brand liquor. I had a friend who insisted on buying the most expensive liquor on the shelf, not only for himself to drink, but to treat his friends. What folly! Who is he trying to impress? If your friends only come to visit your house to drink your expensive liquor, get rid of them. They are not your friends. Alcohol is a **short term status** purchase. It has no utility value. It has no longevity value. It has no appreciation value (unless it is a fine wine, but that's pretty chancy.)

And it's getting more and more expensive every day. When I have been in severe financial crisis, I have stopped serving liquor to my friends entirely. I warned them: "Bring your own." I cooked solid, cheap, delicious food for them, but no liquor. As it turns out, people in Princeton routinely bring a bottle of wine as a gift for the hostess anyway. So it worked out fine. I have been known to keep some of those bottles of expensive wine and take them as gifts to my own hostesses. Well, there's cheap and then there's *very* cheap. However, I haven't noticed a loss of friends over this behavior.

Two areas where you can spend a fortune and have very little to show for it: weddings and funerals.

I have been married twice, and my two weddings were more fun than the two marriages. Both times, I got married at home: first in a little converted chicken coop, 3 room house in San Francisco, and second in my in-laws old Victorian home. The first time I wore a made over dress that had belonged to my mother. The second time, I made my own dress. The first time, my husband bought bunches of flowers at the flower stands on the street corner. The second time, the flowers came out of my mother-in-law's garden and a few from the local florist. No more than twenty people at each wedding, but both weddings fun, relaxing, and delightful. A sharing experience. Because there was so little effort involved, no one was exhausted and angry. No one went bankrupt. We all had time to be together with people we loved, over a home cooked wedding feast beautifully served. I shall never forget my two weddings regardless of what happened afterwards, because they were such fun and also rather funny.

Nowadays, you can take the money you spend on a wedding and have a down payment on a house. Ten thousand dollars on a wedding is not unusual, and what a waste! What kind of value is that? The expensive weddings I've attended have been hectic, rushed, exhausting affairs, where no one really got to spend time with anyone else. The food was overcooked, over fancy, and basically nauseating. The band was so loud, you were deafened. Who needs this?

The same with funerals. I remember when my grandfather was dying, he discussed his funeral with my mother. She called up a mortuary that had handled the funeral of my great grandmother. She told the man over the phone that she wanted "the cheapest funeral they had." He said, "Now, you don't want to be that way." She said, "Yes I do, and hung up." Again, as with everything in this book, funerals are a question of "values," but I emphasize that values may or may not have anything to do with money spent. I have been to one Jewish funeral, which struck me as a sane way to go: a wooden coffin, a memorial service, and burial within a day. No big black limousines. No banks of flowers or a flower car.

My mother asked to be cremated, and her ashes are scattered in a little boot hill cemetery in the mountains of Colorado that she loved.

It is not mercenary to calculate money when planning wedding or funerals. It is mercenary and materialistic to plan weddings and funerals to impress people, to show off, to prove that you have the money to do it, to make it the biggest and the best. False pride should have no place in these events. Status should not attend, only people you love in a sharing environment.

How can I summarize this chapter on shopping? Start with WHAT YOU LOVE and then aim for longevity and utility. Try to eliminate status and prestige from your thinking. It's costly, almost a complete waste of money. You can look good without being broke. You can definitely feel good, get real pleasure, without spending heaps of money. That's the trick.

When you shop, return to those stores or catalogue mail order houses that have consistently given you quality for your money. Stick with them. Nearly every time I've been suckered into going for something "cheaper", I've been stung by poor quality. That is no economy.

CHAPTER EIGHT: TOOLS

Throughout this book, my primary message has been that if you want to get ahead financially, you must do two things: first, wherever possible, substitute your time for your money, and second, to spend money on **capital goods** rather than **consumer goods**. In order to do-it-yourself, you will need tools, and tools are **capital investments**. That is, they are pieces of equipment in which you must invest in order to make more money. The best tools are those you can use over and over and over again, so that their initial cost goes down because it is spread over many years of usage. Some of the tools I am going to discuss below might strike you as peculiar, as not really being tools, but anything that you can use repeatedly to make money for yourself are types of tools or **capital equipment**.

HEALTH TOOLS

Economically, your body and your brains are the most important tools you own. To keep them functioning, you've got to care for them and to do this, you will need to educate yourself about maintaining your health. You can never be too healthy. If you abuse your body, sooner or later it will catch up with you in the form of expensive medical care, time lost from work, lower energy levels to cope with your daily life. Living effectively in today's complicated world takes a lot of energy.

Health care costs have escalated beyond anyone's reach if they do not have health insurance, and even with health insurance, sick people are being forced to pay a greater proportion of their own medical bills. In the area of health care, an ounce of prevention is surely worth more than a pound of cure. For example, it is estimated that for each one dollar spent on immunization against childhood diseases $10 in future medical costs will be saved, that for each one dollar spent on pre-natal care, $3.38 will be saved in medical treatments during the first year of a baby's life. (Source: "*Business Week*," 1992 Special Bonus Issue, p. 104.)

The building blocks of good health include sound nutrition, exercise, rest and enjoyment of life. These building blocks rest upon each other. You cannot enjoy your life if your body is tired from lack of rest, flabby from lack of exercise, debilitated from poor diet. On the other hand, doctors now recognize the value of enjoyment and pleasure in maintaining one's health. A healthy, happy brain leads to a healthier body.

Eating nutritiously is a bit more complicated than you might think at first. The Federal Government publishes dietary guidelines which are a good start. These dietary guidelines are:

Eat no more than 30% of your daily calories in fat.
For women, drink no more than one glass of alcohol per day.
Men can drink two because of their usually greater body weight.
Eat between 3 - 5 servings of vegetables every day, one cup of which should be raw, leafy green vegetables.
Eat between 2 -4 servings of fruit per day.
Eat between 6 - 11 servings of pasta, cereals, breads per day.
Eat between 2 - 3 servings of milk or milk products per day.
Eat between 2- 3 two to three ounce servings of meat, poultry, fish, or eggs per day.

(Source: *The World Almanac and Book of Facts, 1992*).

The sole nutritional concern for many people revolves around fats and cholesterol rather than developing and following a total nutrition and preventive health care program. Much nutritional information published in magazines and newspapers focuses on cholesterol rather than on a total diet plan. Despite its bad press, cholesterol is an important nutrient in one's body, and heart disease results from more than cholesterol intake. Certainly, good health demands more from a diet than watching one's fat intake. I have seen people who worry about their cholesterol continue to eat shabby diets: diets deficient in fresh fruits and vegetables, diets containing too much salt, and too much alcohol. They skip breakfasts or snack on crackers and coffee. They fail to get enough exercise. This is not good preventive health care.

A second prominent concern for many people regarding food intake is weight control. While keeping one's weight under control is very important for overall health, if you restrict your calories too severely in order to keep your weight down, you could be depriving your body of nutrients needed to maintain good health unless you add vitamin and mineral supplements.

The only way to solve the complexities of proper nutrition and health maintenance for yourself is to read and to read widely. Educate yourself. Most women's magazines publish articles on nutrition, as do most newspapers. Read them. Cut them out. Save them for future reference.

There are now several nutrition and health magazines on newsstands. To determine which health magazines you might wish to subscribe to, consult those in your local library, which usually displays two or three common health and nutrition magazines. Find one that rings true to you, that you find easy to read and to understand. Over time, as you become more familiar with the issues surrounding good nutrition, you will begin to trust the information from one source more than from another.

Another excellent source of nutrition information is your local health food store. These stores usually stock racks of books and pamphlets on nutritional approaches to preventing or alleviating many illnesses and health problems.

When you begin to notice the variety of nutritional information out there, you will also notice that there are wide differences of opinion on nutrition. Some doctors and health professionals say that if you eat a "balanced diet", you have nothing to worry about. Others say that eating a balanced diet is not enough, that vitamin and mineral supplementation are required.

There are well over 40 nutrients necessary for good health. The number keeps increasing every year as more research is done. For some nutrients, even scientists do not know what the actual requirements are for optimum human health. Most ordinary people do not have the foggiest notion of what these nutrients are or of what the recommended amounts for health might be. They also do not know in what foods the various nutrients occur. This is why doctors and others recommend the "balanced diet" approach, which assumes that by choosing a wide variety of foods, cooking them properly, and consuming them that people will remain healthy.

This approach contains some inherent flaws, however. Many nutrients are destroyed by heat during cooking, by exposure to air, by the processing done by the food industry. Fruits and vegetables are seasonal, and during the winter, availability is poor. The soils on which foods grow are often depleted of essential minerals and nutrients. Some additives and chemicals used to preserve foods can be harmful to one's health. Different people may have trouble absorbing certain nutrients due to digestive disturbances or food allergies. Some people may be under higher levels of stress which causes them to use nutrients more rapidly. Some types of medication cause people to need some nutrients at higher levels than if they were not taking medication. Thus, the balanced diet approach may not work for many groups of people.

To test your knowledgeability about the nutrients necessary for human health, get out a piece of paper and list every *nutrient* necessary for human health that you can think of. Then compare your list with the one below and opposite. To keep it easier for you, I will not ask you to also list the foods in which these nutrients occur, nor will I ask you whether you eat enough of these foods to insure that you obtain the optimal amount of nutrients, but these are all things you need to know.

NUTRIENTS
- Carbohydrates
- Proteins
- Fats

VITAMINS
- Vitamin A
- Thiamine (B-1)
- Riboflavin (B-2_
- Niacin, Niacinamide, Nicotinic Acid (B-3)
- Pantothenic Acid (B-5)
- Pyridoxine (B-6)
- Cyanocobalamin (B-12)

- Biotin
- Choline
- Folic Acid
- Inositol
- Para-aminobenzoic Acid
- Vitamin C
- Vitamin D
- Vitamin E
- Vitamin K
- Bioflavonoids
- Coenzyme Q-10
- Vitamin F - essential fatty acids

MINERALS

- Boron
- Calcium
- Chromium (Glucose Tolerance Factor)
- Cobalt
- Copper
- Germanium
- Iodine
- Iron
- Magnesium
- Manganese
- Molybdenum
- Phosphorus
- Potassium
- Selenium
- Silicon
- Sodium
- Sulfur
- Vanadium
- Zinc

AMINO ACIDS -- Approximately 29 commonly known

ENZYMES, which occur in raw foods, include digestive and metabolic enzymes.

- Amylase
- Protease
- Lipase

Superoxide dismutase
Catalase
Pancreatin
Papain
Bromelin
Pepsin
Trypsin
Rennin
Chymotrypsin

FIBER
WATER

(Source: *Prescription for Nutritional Healing*, by James F. Balch, M.D. and Phyllis A. Balch, C.N.C., Avery Publishing Group, 1990.)

You are the best judge of whether the "balanced diet" approach is right for you or whether you need additional vitamin and mineral supplementation. Your body will tell you by how you feel. Are you sleeping better? Do you have fewer skin problems? Can you maintain your weight more readily? Do you suffer less from hay fever or seasonal colds and flu? Do you have fewer aches and pains?

Although doctors are seen as the final authority on questions of health, most of them have never studied nutrition as part of their medical training. They may know less about it than you do. Doctors are trained to "treat" sickness. They often know very little about prevention beyond what I have listed above: eat well, rest, exercise. Don't smoke and drink. Don't take drugs. Eat less fat. Only twice have I ever had a doctor inquire into my nutrition: my gynecologist, after many years, asked me if I was "getting enough calcium," and another doctor recommended that I eat a pint of plain yogurt daily while taking antibiotics. Since then I have *never* had a doctor inquire into my eating habits.

I read recently about a case where a woman had undergone several major surgical operations for uncontrolled internal bleeding. Finally one doctor asked her questions about what she ate. He learned that she never ate any fresh fruits or vegetables, and he learned that she was suffering from scurvy--a vitamin C deficiency disease.

Let me give you an example of how nutrition education helps in day to day living. I have mentioned before a young woman who worked for me who had three children. When she placed two of these youngsters in a day care center in Princeton, they began to suffer from diarrhea and nausea during the day. This woman and her children were African Americans. I asked her to check with the day care center to see whether they were feeding those children milk during the day. Sure enough, the children were given milk and graham crackers for morning and afternoon breaks. I suggested to this mother that she ask the day care center to feed the children juice instead of milk. She did and they did. The nausea and diarrhea ceased.

I had read that African Americans and Jews are particularly prone to milk allergies. I have a Jewish friend who used to drink milk in his coffee every morning. By noon he suffered from foul breath and serious gas. When he stopped drinking milk in his coffee and on his cereal, these problems disappeared.

These kinds of health problems may not be particularly serious and not worth visiting a doctor about, but they can cause considerable misery and discomfort in one's life. Through your knowledge of nutrition, you can begin to alleviate some of these problems and prevent unnecessary visits to your doctor.

I used to sleep about 12 hours a day. I was so tired all the time, I could hardly work. One doctor I visited simply said there was nothing the matter with me; I should just sleep more and get more exercise.

I consulted another doctor. He recommended a six hour glucose tolerance test. During the fourth hour of the test, I could hardly keep my head up. My eyes blurred. I could not think or respond to the questions of the nurse. This doctor said that I suffered from hypoglycemia, an illness which some doctors still refuse to recognize as a real illness. However, this doctor gave me no recommendations for treating the illness except for "Go buy some books about it and read them." At that time the primary treatment was a high protein, high fat, low carbohydrate diet. I followed the diet religiously, and within six months, my knees and ankles ached so badly, I could hardly walk.

I read every nutrition book I could find, and learned that a high protein diet is also very high in phosphorus, which in turn drains the calcium out of your bones. I started supplementing my diet with calcium and also with zinc tablets, and within a few weeks, all joint pain disappeared. Since then, the recommended diet for hypoglycemia has been totally changed to a high complex carbohydrate, low fat, low protein diet. I learned of these changes through reading nutrition books and magazines. I did not learn any of this from my doctors.

People differ biochemically. One person can drink milk with no problem at all. Others cannot. Some people are allergic to oranges. I am. Some people are allergic to dogs and cats. Some people get colds every winter that hang on for weeks. Others merely get the sniffles. Because of this biochemical diversity, you are in the best position to decide what is best for your body. Your doctor can advise you and consult with you, but you are the one living inside your skin, not your doctor.

I am not suggesting that you stop seeing your doctor. I am suggesting that *prevention* of illness is your responsibility, not your doctor's. You can prevent many health problems by following this advice: eat well, rest, exercise regularly, and study up on nutrition and preventive health care for you and your children.

In my lifetime, many illnesses that used to be seen as part of growing old or simply part of life have now been found to relate to poor eating habits. Research continues to shed more light on these relationships. Recently beta-carotene has been hailed as important in certain forms of cancer prevention. Much adult onset diabetes can be controlled through proper diet, weight loss and vigorous exercise. Bowel diseases can be alleviated by adding more fiber to one's diet. Health problems peculiar to women--premenstrual syndrome and symptoms associated with menopause--can often be reduced through proper diet and nutrition. Certainly, a quality diet is absolutely essential if you are to give birth to healthy children.

COOKING TOOLS

The human body is a bit like a computer: garbage in, garbage out. Now that you've decided to stop putting garbage into your body, to eat nutritiously, how do you learn to prepare good food. Get a cookbook. I prefer the *Fannie Farmer Cookbook* because at the beginning of each chapter, it gives an overview or summary of the principles involved in preparing those foods. For example, at the beginning of the chapter on "Meat", the book describes the various ways of cooking meat such as roasting, broiling, grilling, pan broiling, sautéing, and stewing and braising. Different cuts and types of meat demand different cooking methods in order to maintain their flavor, their tenderness and their nutrition. When you learn the basic principles of cooking, rather than just following a recipe, you can cook many things without any kind of recipe. If you understand that flour always dissolves in cold liquids or hot fats, you will never have lumpy gravy.

When you know the basic principles of making soup or stock, you can always make your own, or take canned soup and improve it. I personally find canned soup too salty and often lacking in really tasty meat or vegetables. Rather than cook a big pot of soup for myself (and there is no such thing as a small pot of homemade soup), I will sauté a little onion, some celery and carrot, add them to a pan of canned soup, throw in leftover meat I may have on hand, perhaps add some Chinese noodles at the last minute, and voila! Good soup! If I have a can of potato soup on hand, I have found that adding my own sautéed green onions, and some of my own boiled potatoes, which I usually have on hand, is a great improvement, and takes only about 5 minutes of my time. A little dollop of sour cream significantly improves the soup, as well as a little dry white wine.

After you've bought a really good cookbook, you will need a **pantry**. The idea of a **pantry** came from my mother. When I say **pantry** I mean a stock of basic food ingredients, the so-called "staples" that underlie all simple cooking. One reason so many people say "I don't have time to cook" is that they do not have the necessary ingredients on hand all the time. If you have your pantry stocked, you can always throw together a good meal in very little time.

Now that I am marooned in the snows of the Colorado Rockies during the winter, I must keep a well-stocked pantry. What is in my pantry?

1. A variety of canned soups and broths to use as base for my own "improved" soup.
2. Flour, sugar, brown sugar, baking powder, baking soda, corn starch and tapioca. I use the tapioca as a thickening agent for pies as well as a quick desert when company arrives unexpectedly. Tapioca pudding with frozen raspberries on top is a treat.
3. Seasonings: my most important are thyme, basil, oregano, cinnamon, ginger, fresh garlic, salt and pepper.
4. A variety of fresh, frozen and canned fruit: bananas, frozen berries, canned peaches and apricots, fresh grapes. I use fruit for desserts often, mixing bothfresh, canned, and frozen to dilute some of the sugar and give a variety of textures and flavors.
5. Canned tuna to make casseroles or sandwiches or salads.
6. A variety of pasta and noodles, Chinese noodles, for salads, or hot pasta dishes.
7. Rice.
8. Several cans of tomato sauce to make pasta dishes, barbecue sauces some kinds of salad dressings. I keep both large and small cans on hand.
9. Oatmeal to use for meat loaf and cereals, as well as cookies.
10. Coffee, tea, cocoa, and both sweet and semi-sweet chocolate to make cakes and cookies and pies.
11. Raisins and pecans. They always spruce up cereals, breads, pancakes, etc.
12. Extra Virgin olive oil and salad oil for salad dressings and cooking.
13. Mayonnaise, Dijon mustard and catsup.
14. Parmesan cheese. Use it on pasta dishes and also as a garnish in broth soups as well as on top of some beef stews with noodles.
15. Beef and chicken bouillon cubes. These enhance soups and gravies, and you can use them to make a hot drink during the snowstorms of winter. Use them in the cooking broth when you make rice.
16. Onions, celery, carrots and fresh potatoes.
17. Frozen peas. They go with anything, and brighten soups and salads.

18. French bread. To keep it fresh, keep it frozen in the freezer until you need it. Buy a big loaf and cut it into three pieces; wrap two of them and freeze them. Keep the third in the refrigerator to use as needed. You can do this with any kind of bread.
19. Frozen hamburger and pieces of chicken to be thawed and used in soups, pasta dishes or as main courses.

I have other things that I routinely keep in my pantry, but these are the most basic. When you stock these ingredients, you can always whip together a tasty meal for yourself, your children, sudden guests. They won't be fancy meals, but flavorful and nutritious.

Cooking utensils

You can't cook without good utensils. You don't need many. I recommend:

1. Three heavy sauce pans: large, medium and small, stainless steel.
2. One big skillet
3. One big heavy bottomed stewing pot or Dutch oven with lids that are oven proof.
4. One stock pot, stainless steel. None of my pots are aluminum. While the evidence is inconclusive, there has been some association between aluminum and Alzheimer's disease. Also, a tomato sauce or a wine sauce or any type of acidic ingredients will cause an aluminum pot to blacken and will leach some of the aluminum into your cooking. At any rate, I simply don't use aluminum to cook in any more.

I use these pots and pans day after day, and have had them for more than 20 years. I have a variety of heavy mixing bowls ranging from small to large. Several measuring cups and measuring spoons. A hand mixer. A grater. A variety of big spoons with big handles so I can get a good grip on them. Sharp knives of all sorts. A whet stone to keep those knives really sharp. A good potato peeler. A wooden chopping board. A meat thermometer and an oven thermometer. These take the guessing out of your baking and roasting.

I have a vast array of baking pans of all sizes, but I bake rarely now. I watch my weight too, as do most of my friends, and cakes and pies rarely show up for dessert. Fruit with custards or puddings works just fine, and these kinds of desserts take less time to prepare.

When planning your meals, think in terms of dinners and lunches, not just a dinner or a lunch. Cook in bulk so that you will have leftovers available for your lunches and other meals. This means you'll have to keep a sharp watch on the contents of your refrigerator so that nothing turns green and moldy, but leftovers provide a much more economical source of lunch foods than those you buy specifically for lunches, such as deli meats and cheeses and prepared deli salads.

For example, when you broil chicken for a dinner, broil enough so that you have leftovers with which to make your lunches. Boil several potatoes at one time, more than you need for a dinner. This saves on the gas or electricity of your stove, and also provides potatoes to drop into soups, to make hash browns which can be served with scrambled eggs either as a dinner or a breakfast. You can cut them up into salads for your lunches. You can heat them in your microwave for dinners. I keep boiled potatoes in their skins in plastic bags in the refrigerator.

HOME MAINTENANCE TOOLS

Even if you live in an apartment, you need tools. The landlord is not always going to be there when you need him. If you decide to string a clothesline rather than buy that expensive rent-to-own dryer, you will need tools. Nowadays, if you buy inexpensive desks and bookcases, you will have to take them home in a box and put them together yourself. This takes tools, at least screw drivers and a hammer.

Many husbands have a set of tools. My husband did. However, he never put his tools were he could find them easily, so he "borrowed" mine, which I kept in a bottom drawer in my kitchen. He never returned them. Now, this was not the only reason for our divorce, but it was a contributing factor. Most women I know have this problem. I have a friend who has even bought a tool box to store her tools in, and her husband still "borrows" them and doesn't return them. If necessary, hide them in your big stock pot, but get your own set of home repair tools. You will need:

A good set of screw drivers, both Phillips and regular.
A pair of pliers. I always need them to unscrew bottle lids now.
A good hammer.
Assorted nails and screws.
A steel tape measure.

An electric drill. This really takes the pain out of mounting shelves or other things on your walls. Get one with a reverse and an assortment of drill bits.

A stud finder. This is the handiest tool, and has saved me more grief. Mine has a battery in it, which allows me to locate a stud in the wall without pounding nails. I thought it was expensive when I bought it, but I wouldn't be without it now.

One or two pipe wrenches. I am not a plumber, but there are times when I must change a faucet washer, and wrenches are a must.

A set of both metric and non-metric hand wrenches.

A good saw. Actually, I have two or three hand saws, and one electric circular saw and a small table saw. That table saw was a terrific investment. It saves so much time and does a much better job than a hand saw. If you have a basement, I recommend getting a table saw. Get a good one. You can get cheap ones for about $125 I think, but when you take them home, you will find that many of the parts are plastic and it will be difficult for you to get the saw blade to set really straight. I think it's worth paying an extra $50 to get a good table saw. I also bought a high quality saw blade for mine. It cuts through wood like butter.

One or two heavy duty extension cords so you can take your electric drill or your electric saw anywhere you need to go.

A level.

I paint the inside of my house often. It saves money. So, I keep spackling compound and putty knives on hand to plug holes in the walls. I own a variety of paintbrushes and rollers, and a couple of really good canvas drop cloths. I have sandpaper to smooth down my spackling.

If you know absolutely nothing about home repairs, go to your local all purpose hardware/home improvement store. They usually have a rack of home improvement books: how to do your own plumbing, simple electric, painting, simple carpentry. I had a Channel Home Center store near me when I lived in New Jersey. I should have owned stock in that company, because it seemed I went there every weekend to stock up on home maintenance and improvement supplies, including pre-cut pieces of lumber.

I am a poor carpenter, but I can whack together a dog house or a hanging bird feeder. I always need to add more shelves in my closets. I have made my own work benches and cupboards to store things. I scavenge pieces of lumber and old cupboards that people put out at the curb for trash collection. I take them home and reuse them to make my own cupboards and storage areas. I used my electric chain saw to cut away part of my deck railing so I could build in a bench to sit on. If you have trees and shrubs at your house, an electric chain saw is a real necessity for cutting up fallen branches. Otherwise a bow saw solves many problems.

If you have a yard or garden, of course you need tools. I am not going to list them here. You will find them as you need them.

NOTE: A good place to buy tools of all kinds is a yard sale, garage sale or flea market. Try not to buy tools new. They are so *cheap* at garage sales. I know. I just sold all of my gardening tools when I moved. It hurt me to sell them so cheap, and when I got out here, despite my best intentions, I found I *must* have a little garden, so I replaced all my tools too expensively.

CLOTHING REPAIR TOOLS

You can save money on clothing if you repair it rather than throwing it away and replacing it. You need needles and thread of various colors, good scissors, and iron on patches. One other thing you will need: a variety of special spot removing detergents or cleaners. I don't know what has happened, but the fabrics used in clothing today absorb grease and tomato sauce so that these spots are nearly impossible to remove. If you take the spotted garment, napkins, or table cloths and apply spot removers immediately, or very quickly, soak them overnight, and then wash them, you have a small prayer of getting the spots out. If you send the garments through a dryer with the spots on, you can forget it. They are there forever.

If you keep needle and thread handy, you can repair that seam around the collar of your turtleneck before it gets larger. You can re-hem the lining of your coat before it tears further. You can patch the knees of your jeans, especially if they are work jeans that suffer the worst forms of abuse. You can sew up the thumbs on your children's mittens.

If you have a $20 turtleneck sweater with a torn seam under the arm, it will take you about ten minutes, at most, to repair it. To calculate the money you earn by mending this turtleneck:

<u>CALCULATION:</u> Divide 10 minutes into 60 (one hour) = 6 x $20 (the amount saved by not having to buy a new sweater), or earning power of about $120 an hour. Do you earn this much at your job?

I think mending has fallen out of fashion. I never see or hear of anyone's doing it anymore. Perhaps it's just the people I know. However, I mend, often. Yes, I get tired of wearing the same old clothes year after year, but not so tired that I want to keep spending money on clothing when I'd rather take a trip to Europe.

Of course, if you follow my advice to sew, you will need a sewing machine. I use an old Singer that my grandmother used to own. It must be fifty years old by now, but it works fine and does what I need it to do, which is mostly to sew seams.

As with the other tools listed above, the important thing is to have a special place or sewing box for all your sewing and mending needs so you can always find them when you need them. How many times have you been ready to step out the door, taken one last turn in the mirror, and seen your hem is down. If you have your sewing box at hand, you can repair that hem immediately.

I have a sewing box given to me over thirty years ago. I keep it stocked with everything I need. God help anyone who takes the scissors out of my sewing box to use for some other activity! I urge you to spend good money for scissors. I have bought many of those cheap ones with the plastic handles, and they have turned out to be utterly worthless.

CAR REPAIR TOOLS

I do not attempt to repair my own car, nor do I change its oil and filters. I could save money this way, but that is one area I simply have decided to leave to others. However, I changed the oil on my lawn tractor when I had one. This saved me about $60 each time I did it: the $25 pick-up and delivery fee that the tractor service center charged plus their labor charges at $30 an hour plus the cost of the oil. Furthermore, by changing the oil myself, and doing it more often, I prevented excess wear and tear on the engine.

Again, to encourage myself to perform this task as needed, I kept a plastic funnel to drain the oil, a plastic bottle to catch the used oil so I could recycle it at the gas station, the appropriate wrench marked with a piece of tape "lawn tractor", and a roll of paper towels in the garage. With these tools handy, plus the quarts of oil I bought at my local supermarket, it was less of a chore to change the oil. Then I marked the date on my calendar, which sat beside my phone in the kitchen. Each month, I changed the oil on the tractor.

STORING YOUR TOOLS

I believe that one reason people do not "do-it-themselves" more often is because they don't keep their tools organized. When I visit my neighbors, I see that their garages, their cellars, their attics are absolutely chaotic. They couldn't find a wrench in that mess if they tried. This definitely discourages one's efforts to do it yourself.

Throughout this book, I have emphasized the trade-off between your time and your money. One of the keys to effective use of your time is to have a place for every tool, and then always keep your tools in their correct place. If you are working outside the home, or inside for that matter, you do not have the time to waste searching for lost tools.

Well, you say, I don't have the room. When I see the attics and garages and cellars and closets of my friends, and talk with them and observe how they live, I see that they don't "throw things away." If you save every piece of garbage you have collected in your life, of course you won't have any room. My motto has been if I don't use it within about two years, I throw it away or give it to someone who will use it. That goes for *everything* , but especially clothes.

My best friend has admitted to me that she has trunks of clothing she will never wear again but which are "too good to throw away." This problem supports my advice to you to "always buy what you love." When you love it, you use it. If you don't love it, get rid of it. There are people in the world desperate for good clothing and household furnishings that you don't need or want. You need space. You need room to cook, room to sew, room to do your own repairs. This is a much more valuable use of space than storage of useless clothing, furniture, toys and other debris of modern living. Toss out that old TV. Give away the old bikes. If the ice skates haven't been used in 5 years, get rid of them. Odd sheets and old towels--get rid of them or use them to clean up after the dog. Broken shovels, bent rakes, plastic pans and buckets that are cracked or partially useless, get rid of them.

If you don't have storage room, add an extra shelf to your closet. Build small cupboards for the inside of the closet or for your garage. Most garages have unused space up toward the roof. Hang shelves up there, and keep a stool or small ladder handy so you can reach them. I keep small stools in all of my closets and in my kitchen so I can reach things I have stored up high off the floor. Hang shelves on the insides of your closet and cupboard doors. Put boxes under your beds.

If your children or other family members tend to steal your tools, buy them a set, and lock yours up. I have found it worth the money to keep a complete set of wrenches and screw drivers both in my kitchen (or cellar) and in my garage. I mount the screw drivers in their little plastic holders onto the wall so they are there whenever I need them. The amount of frustration and running around it saves to have a set of screwdrivers in two or more places is unimaginable. You can buy a set of screwdrivers for less than $10.

I have found that keeping tools in a plastic bucket is a big help. If I want to hang a shelf in my upstairs, I simply load my bucket and take everything with me. I mean everything I could possibly use, because it never fails that you will need whatever tool you left downstairs.

A tile repairman once came to my house, and he kept all his tools in a 5 gallon plastic bucket that had once been used to hold spackling compound. Those 5 gallon buckets are worth their weight in gold. I always keep 3 or 4 around. Often you can find them lying along the highway, or on the curb waiting for trash collection, or in the dumpsters at a construction site. Stop, pick them up, and clean them up. They have a hundred uses.

In addition to his 5 gallon bucket, the tileman's wife had sewn a sort of apron, with all kinds of pockets in it which hung around the sides of the bucket. He kept all of his tools in this bucket and never had to search for them when he needed them. I have seen that you can buy those "bucket aprons" now.

OFFICE TOOLS

Today's world gets more and more complicated. You've got to keep records of nearly everything. You need to make notes to remind yourself to do things. You need to fight over bills that are not accurate. You need to file your canceled checks for tax purposes. To do this, you need some sort of desk or office and you need office supplies. When you have the necessary paper, envelopes, a dictionary, and a good typewriter, you will be more inclined to fight over inaccurate billings, to argue over inappropriate charges, to pursue people to get refunds or to get action on product warranties.

Recently, my bank charged me fees for transactions that resulted from a mistake they had made. I sat down and typed off an angry letter, explaining what had happened and telling them that I resented paying my money for their mistakes. I didn't really think it would make any difference, but because I had the tools handy, I sat down and did it. It took me about ten minutes. A few days later, my bank sent me a letter telling me that they were crediting my account with $20 to cover some of the fees. For ten minutes of my time, I earned $20. That is an hourly rate of $120. (10 minutes divided into 60 = 6 x $20 = $120.)

You can buy a good electric typewriter for about $125. Unfortunately electric typewriters nowadays take disposable ribbons. This is one of those **hidden costs** I've mentioned above. The ribbons cost about $5.00 or so, and it seems to me that they do not last very long. You can buy electric typewriters with cloth ribbons. In the long run, I believe this would be more economical, but it makes correcting your errors a bit more inconvenient.

I believe a typewriter is absolutely essential when writing business letters. It insures that your message will be legible and also allows you to make copies, using carbon paper, of all your correspondence, an essential means of recalling exactly what happened and when.

If you don't know how to type, I suggest you buy a book and teach yourself. Learning to type is an example of the value of continuing education. Earlier when I emphasized education as an economic asset, being able to type was an example in my mind. You can take typing classes at many adult schools if you do not wish to try to teach yourself. If you type well, you will always be able to get a job. In today's world, typing is a skill that will serve you for the rest of your life. My father now suffers from such severe arthritis that he can no longer write. If he could type, he could communicate and handle his business affairs. He could write his memoirs. He would have a means of expressing himself that would alleviate his boredom and loneliness.

My cousin's father is nearly blind. If he could type, he could communicate and express himself and help pass the long days that he now spends sitting in a chair, alone and bored. If you have children in school, they should all take typing classes. To be unable to type rapidly is to be seriously impaired for participation in tomorrow's job market. This is a computer world. If you can type, you can use a computer. These machines can open up new worlds for you and your children, but you must know how to type, at least somewhat, in order to use them.

After you get your typewriter, you will need a ream of typing paper. Paper comes in a variety of weights and colors. When you buy typing paper, do not confuse it with "copying" paper or paper suitable for laser printers. This latter type of paper has a special coating on it and is more expensive than regular white typing paper.

I buy carbon paper sets to make copies of *every* letter I send when I'm arguing with the bank, a department store, the federal government or whatever. I do not have a copier handy, and sometimes I want to get the letter into the mail immediately. Carbon paper saves me some time and some money. Most copies cost about 8 - 10 cents, but with carbon paper, a copy is only one or two cents.

You will also find it helpful to keep some 9 x 12 brown envelopes on hand and a box of labels that you can paste on these envelopes so you can type clearly legible addresses rather than hand writing them.

A Rolodex address file is easier to keep up-to-date than the little book types. You can just toss the old cards away and retype the new address on a new card.

You will need a calendar for the current year as well as one showing the past year or two and the next year.

Buy batches of cheap, disposable ball-point pens and always keep them everywhere in the house along with small yellow lined tablets.

You can buy stamps in batches of 20 to keep on hand.

You will need a good stapler and staples. When I type a letter in response to one sent to me, I staple the two together and file them so I have a complete record of the correspondence.

FILES

Keeping up-to-date files is an absolute necessity in today's complicated world. You will need some manila filing folders and some sort of cardboard box in which to put your files. If you work in an office where they throw out used manila folders, retrieve them and put new labels on them. I have done this often. For a file, any old box will do if it's about the size of 9 x 12 paper or manila folders. Go to an instant printing store or copying store and ask for one of the boxes that their reams of paper come in. These are an excellent size and very strong.

The files you will need include:

Warranty files

With every appliance or product you buy, you usually receive some sort of warranty and often some sort of information booklet about proper operation of the product. You must keep these records. File them in the manila folders under appropriate headings: "stove, microwave, VCR, TV, washer, dryer, CD player, answering machine." If you are like me, you have trouble remembering how to use some of your equipment or appliances. I can never remember how to clean my chain saw. I must keep the instructions handy in a "chain saw" file so that I can refresh my memory. This is true for most appliances. Nowadays, you are responsible for keeping them clean and in good working order. Calling an appliance repair man is too expensive if you can do-it-yourself.

Insurance files

You will need files for your automobile insurance, automobile registration, homeowners insurance and all medical insurance and medical bills.

Job files

A particularly important file you will need is one that holds copies of job references or recommendations you have received and a complete record of all the jobs you have held, with the dates of employment. I cannot emphasize this enough. If you do not work outside the home, but you do volunteer work, keep copies of what you have done, who you worked with, the actual tasks you performed. Do you organize the church suppers? Do you arrange the church flowers? Are you on a committee at your children's school? Keep a record of these jobs with names of people you can contact to give you references if you need them in the future.

You will not remember what you have done in your job or career or the various activities you have handled in your off hours. Time goes by and you forget, or worse, you think that what you have done "doesn't matter" or that it was unimportant. Never think that! You cannot anticipate when a job will come along that you especially want, one that demands skills you used as a volunteer but did not actually use in your previous job. You will not remember the names and addresses of people who can help you unless you keep these records. You will forget the volunteer activities you have done.

One reason for keeping records for *every* job or task is that if you want to shift jobs or careers, you need to be able to prove to prospective employers that you have skills in the new area. For women, this is especially important. At one time, I was very discouraged with my career in market research. I went to an employment agency and told the man that I wanted to "do something different." I had no evidence that I could do anything different. He bluntly told me that if I did not want to continue in market research, he would not handle me as a client.

There is a myth out there and it's called "transferable skills". Companies give lip service to the idea that skills and talents can be transferred to different types of jobs, but in fact, most organizations want to slot you and keep you in that slot. It makes their lives easier. The only way you can change the type of work you do, to transfer into a new career, is either to get more education, or acquire new skills outside of your job which can be used to show your competency in a new field. For this, you will need to keep very good records and references of these skills to take with you to new job interviews.

For example, I was president of my homeowner's association. This is not a big deal, but it does show some management skill, some organizational experience. I was the only woman on the board, so it demonstrated my ability to work with men effectively. I know that I could ask the other board members for a recommendation if I needed one. I was on the board of trustees of my local church, which handled the long range financial planning and the investments of the church. This job, again not a big deal, showed my willingness to volunteer and some familiarity with investment decision making. These types of activities count if you are looking for a new job after not having worked for several years.

Keep records of your experience and skills in every activity or job you undertake, and keep an up-to-date record of the names and addresses of *everyone* you have worked with, in whatever capacity. These people can provide a network of information that will help you find a new job and provide recommendations to potential employers. In today's competitive job market, this is the primary way people find good jobs, because most good jobs are not advertised in the local newspapers.

Keep copies of your resume, and keep your resume up-to-date. You've just received a promotion at your job, with new responsibilities--make a note of that on your resume. An important indicator of your skills is the number of times you have been promoted.

If you work outside the home, keep copies of your job performance reviews at your home with the names and addresses of fellow employees or supervisors with whom you have worked who could give you references or recommendations if you need to find another job.

Keep copies of examples of your skills: particular reports you prepared that were especially difficult or that show how competent you are. I suggest that you keep these records at home, because "pink slips" are often given out on Fridays. You don't know when you might be laid off and unable to return to your desk or office. If there are political upheavals at your office, you may not be able to take your files and records with you when you leave. Therefore, take them with you little by little on a weekly or daily basis so that regardless of what happens at your office, you have the necessary copies and information at your home.

In my closet at home, I kept several different types of resumes on file. A resume for a teaching job, a resume for a marketing job, a resume for a newsletter editing job.

I kept a history of my job experience with dates of employment, names of clients who would give me a good recommendation if I wanted a different job.

I kept copies of all the newsletters I edited and wrote for a volunteer arts organization. I may never apply for a job as a newsletter editor, but if I do, I have examples of my work.

A few years ago, I taught in a program for disadvantaged students in Trenton. I kept copies of all the teaching materials I designed and developed for that class so that if I wanted to apply for another teaching job, I could show what I had done that was original, innovative and competent.

I kept boxes of questionnaires I had designed and reports that I had written, so that if I wanted to move to a different marketing research organization, I could take examples of my work to show my competency.

I have always kept a copy of my college transcript.

Tax records

After job records, the most important record keeping you will ever do is for the Internal Revenue Service. I am not going into a lot of detail about this problem, but you must keep records to document the data in your federal tax returns. One of the major expenses of tax return preparation is that people do not keep good records, and their accountants must sort through heaps of papers brought in shoe boxes to their offices. Tax accountants charge anywhere from $100 to $200 an hour to do your taxes. Spending this money to sort through boxes of papers because you have been too lazy to file them in an orderly fashion is a waste of your money.

Every year, I label a manila folder with the current tax year: "IRS 1993," or "IRS 1994." Each time I make a tax deductible donation, I throw the receipt in that file. I keep copies of my property tax payments in that file. At the end of the year, I stuff all my 1099 forms (those that report interest and dividends paid to me) in that file. I put my W-2 copies in it. When the IRS sends my tax forms, I put them in it.

I own my home, so whenever I make a capital improvement, I record it on sheets of paper that I file under "Capital Improvements List." These expenses are deductible when you sell your homes at a profit. Although you may not declare a capital gain until you sell your last home or when you hit age 55, you must be able to document all of your capital improvements on every house you have ever owned. This lowers your tax liability. It saves you money. Keep these records forever. When you die, your executor may need this information.

When my mother died, I was forced to handle the paperwork. She had done all the record keeping and paperwork during their marriage, and my father knew very little about it. They owned four houses at her death. When I began to sort through her "files," I found scraps of paper with scrawled notes on them about how much she had paid someone to add new gutters, or install the hot water heaters, to build the new porches. I could not decipher half of this. I could not determine which house received which capital improvement. I could not sort out what was a capital improvement and what was a repair, which is not tax deductible. When we sold those houses, I am sure we lost money because my mother's records were impossible for me to read.

Other files

I keep copies of my MasterCard statements because they help document the purchase of office supplies, reference materials, and books that I use in my private business of writing. I need these records to document my expenses on my tax returns.

Fire records

You should keep records, in a safe place away from your home, of your purchases of tools, home furnishings and valuables that you may replace in case of fire. My ex-husband had a cellar full of the most expensive tools of all kinds. I don't believe he had any complete record of them, but to replace them, even at depreciated value, would cost an immense amount of money. The insurance company will not reimburse him for those tools unless he can document that he had them. The only way he can be sure of being reimbursed in case of fire is if he can provide receipts or records or photographs.

I keep a complete list of all my antiques and jewelry, with receipts or canceled checks, in my safe deposit box in case of fire. I have some pictures of my most valuable antiques and rugs.

One further type of record keeping or filing: I believe that every wife should keep her own copies of the household federal tax returns. This is especially true if she is in a difficult or unhappy marriage. I know of a woman whose husband came into the house while she was away with her children at a birthday party. He took every shred of paper that would document his earning power, and hid it away from her so she had no way of proving what he earned when they subsequently went into divorce proceedings. If you do not have copies of your joint tax returns, you will have a difficult if not impossible task trying to prove what your husband earns and what your assets are in order to assure that you get your share. If you must pay a lawyer to locate these kinds of files, it can cost you thousands of dollars, which you cannot afford. Rather than keep your copies in your home where your husband can find them, you may find it advisable to store them at your desk at work or at the home of a trusted friend or in your own private safe deposit box.

This squirreling away of tax returns for your future economic safety may sound a bit disgusting to you. It certainly sounds as though you don't "trust" your husband. Believe me, you do not know when you may end up divorced, and when that happens, blind trust in your husband's honor can destroy you economically. The same thing is true if you are widowed. Ignorance of your spouse's financial affairs can spell financial disaster for you.

I recently received a letter from a friend of mine. In it she wrote about the problems her aunt has had since her uncle had a stroke. My friend writes: "My aunt is an intelligent and very interesting woman. She is the image of a true European 'lady' from a bygone era. At the time of my visit, my uncle, who had always handled the finances, was recovering from a stroke. Prior to my uncle's illness, aside from using credit cards and writing checks, my aunt never dealt with or thought about their finances. She didn't even know how much money they had. While I was there, I helped her with insurance forms which had been returned because of insufficient information. She was totally overwhelmed by all the papers and instructions. I made the necessary phone calls, found out what was missing and took care of it for her. It was a simple task for me because I've worked in the business world and know how to maneuver. To her, it was unmanageable. A week after my visit, my uncle passed away."

If I can convince you that the myths of "romance" and "image" and "glamour" and "feminine" have no place in your economic planning, I will consider this book a success. Even if your husband loves you, is honorable, and genuinely caring, you must not let him take away your financial independence and financial management skills. It is a trap. I have fallen into such a situation and paid for it dearly.

I will not discuss THE HOME OFFICE further. I hope I've made my point. You need to keep records systematically and constantly. To do this, you need files. You need the materials available to cope with this complex world. As with your other tools, you need an accessible place for your files, and then you will maintain them. Properly maintained files save you time and save you money. Ultimately, they can save your entire economic life.

In summary, to carry out your plan of financial gain, you will need the necessary tools. Many of these tools are a **capital investment**, that is you must spend money to make money. You must buy these tools, and they will in turn earn more money for you. If you do not have the money to buy tools, ask your friends and relations to give tools to you for Christmas and birthdays, and other holidays. If you have neighbors where the husband has a lot of tools, and he dies, ask if you can purchase the tools from his widow if she does not need them.

My last husband had no shame about such things. He was a telephone installer, and as a result he got to snoop around in people's cellars when he installed their phones. If he saw some tools that were obviously not being used, tools that he could use, he asked to buy them. Almost always, he got them, and got them cheap. I found one of my best wrenches lying in the middle of a highway. I stopped to pick it up. I also picked up a padded movers blanket lying alongside the highway. Don't be embarrassed to scavenge in people's trash. I've done it often. One of the country's wealthiest bag women. That's me.

SECTION THREE: YOUR MONEY AND YOUR EMOTIONS

CHAPTER NINE: YOUR MONEY, HIS MONEY

Throughout this book, I have discussed the handling of money and the various financial concepts as objectively as possible. However, despite the best intentions, women handle money emotionally. Men also handle money emotionally although they may not admit it. The most blatant example of male emotion and money is a man's insistence on handling the money even if his wife is smarter at the task. For men, money is power. In our country we judge the success of men by their ability to earn and keep large amounts of money under their control.

Whether you wish to believe it or not, the same holds true for women. Women who have money have power. Poor women and poor children are the most powerless groups in our society. Unfortunately, rich women are often the brunt of male sexist jokes. Men, and women too, fear and resent powerful women, but that should not stop you from doing everything you can to become wealthy. Poor women are the brunt of sexist jokes too. I would rather be rich and the brunt of jokes than poor and the brunt of jokes.

If you are married and you begin to acquire wealth, it may disrupt your marriage. I know of a young woman who is highly valued by her employer. He recently raised her wages to $60,000 a year. She was the only person in his company to receive both a major pay raise and a bonus this year, a year which has been financially difficult for the company. This woman's husband earns less than $20,000 a year. Neither one of them has a college education. They experienced some very rocky times as her salary burgeoned way beyond his. His pride was wounded by her success, but they have worked things out, and now he is able to take pride in her achievements.

It has always amazed me that a man's pride is wounded by a wife's financial success, but a woman's pride is not supposed to be wounded by the success of her husband. I have finally reached the stage in my life where if a man resents my success, I tell him to get out of my life. His exit makes room for men who enjoy my company because I am successful, interesting, and dynamic.

In addition to fear of male ridicule for being too masculine, women let love influence their financial decisions, but unfortunately love, loyalty, faithfulness, selflessness, all these "feminine" virtues can keep you poor if you let them affect how you handle your money. So, you need to determine when it makes *financial good sense* to share your assets, your bank accounts, your money. By share, I mean having your assets and bank accounts in joint names rather than in your name and his name individually.

One example of the unfortunate financial role of love in a marriage is joint bank accounts. I suppose a joint bank account is an outward and visible sign of an inward, invisible state: a partnership of love. Even then, I don't see any *financial* advantages to a joint bank account, and there are financial *disadvantages* to joint accounts. Perhaps I'm a cynic.

There are advantages to having a home in joint name, particularly if you are a full time housewife and this is the only major asset in the marriage. Having control over half of the major asset gives you some negotiating power in a divorce proceeding, but joint bank accounts fulfill psychological needs, not economic needs.

The problem with a joint bank account is that I have rarely met a man who did not think that what was his was his, and what was yours was negotiable. When you have money in your own name, separate from that of the man in your life, you have financial freedom. I know of marriages where the husband tyrannizes his wife because he has money and she does not. Psychologically, not having money makes a woman feel dependent, and in fact, she is dependent.

Recently, I met a young woman who told me that before her marriage, her lover accommodated her, yielded to her wishes, seemed completely amenable to sharing their assets. As soon as they married, he changed. He did not want her to leave the house except to go grocery shopping. He forbade her to socialize with friends and neighbors. She was to stay home to care for the children. He doled out an allowance to her, one that was so meager she had to draw on her own savings, which came from a previous inheritance, to purchase games and toys for their children. He kept his financial affairs a complete secret from her, but she suspected he was stockpiling money in his own accounts where she could not find it. This man used his earning power, his job, his money as a club over his wife. Since she had no outside income except from her inheritance, she had no way of effectively combating him.

I have a friend who is seriously considering a divorce from her husband of fifty years. His first line of attack is, "I won't let you have any of the money." Fortunately for her, present laws in this state allow equitable distribution of marital assets in a divorce proceeding, but she may still not get as much as half of the household assets if they split up.

As discussed earlier, the first important reason for holding a paying job outside the home is to become financially independent if you are divorced or widowed or never marry. A second good reason is to prevent the tyranny of a husband who thinks his earning power entitles him to rule the roost, to keep his wife completely under his control. The overall goal of having money in your own name, under your own control is to have a means of paying for a life of your own that is not dependent on the good will of any man, except perhaps your boss.

Several years ago, one of my sisters-in-law left her husband and came to stay with me for two weeks because she did not have a dime to her name. All the household money was in her husband's checking account, and he gave her an allowance, which she had already spent for that week. She had never held a job outside the home, and had nowhere to turn because *she had no money of her own.*

There are important advantages to having your own accounts beyond simple personal control. They help establish your own credit rating, your own credit history. Even then, you'll find yourself in some difficulty if you get divorced or widowed. When I was married, I had my own Visa card, in my name alone. I had opened it, and I was the only one who ever used it. I paid all the bills with my own personal checks. I had a $5,000 line of credit on that card. When I divorced, I asked for a new card number because in a previous marriage, my ex-husband had charged on my cards and the bills had come to me. When

I received my new card, my line of credit had been lowered to $500. I was so incensed, I canceled the card and have never used a Visa card since.

If you have children from a previous marriage and all your assets are held jointly in a second marriage, if you die, your spouse will receive all the assets, leaving your children with nothing. He could remarry, have a new family and leave all of your assets as well as his to his new family.

If you have your own accounts and your own assets, you are a more powerful adversary in a divorce proceeding. Despite major changes in the past twenty years, it is still a man's world. Chances are you will be dealing with male lawyers and male judges. Unless you have the image and power that go with control of your own assets, you will be seen as a "dependent female" by the legal system. Your value as a human being will not equal that of your spouse, who is male.

You think I am joking? During my last divorce, my husband selected a lawyer who saw that there were big bucks to be made in drawing out the proceedings. Keep in mind that lawyers make money by charging by the hour. The more work they can create for themselves, the more money they will earn. In a divorce this translates often, but not always, into a lawyer's deliberately stoking the fires of hurt and anger that naturally accompany a breaking marriage. The man and the woman become so angry with one another, that they fight instead of negotiate their way through the divorce. A bitterly contested divorce costs more money in legal fees than if you and your husband can settle it amicably.

At the time of my last divorce, although New Jersey had an equitable distribution law and no fault divorce, this lawyer assured my husband that *all* of the assets in this marriage were legally and fairly his, which was a lie, but my husband was ignorant, and he accepted what this unscrupulous lawyer told him at face value. Our assets included six houses (five were rentals), my share of an inheritance, my share of the company I had founded as well as all the cash and investments.

Because of the inequity in the federal tax laws at that time regarding distribution of property from wives to husbands at death, I held three houses in my name and my husband had three houses in his. I had my own savings and checking accounts, as did my husband. We had a joint account only for the rental income from the properties. Since I handled all the bookkeeping, I knew what my husband had in his accounts, but he never paid any attention to what I had in mine.

As we sat around the table, my husband's lawyer learned about this state of affairs, and he was absolutely astonished. He looked at me, and asked in slight outrage, "Why do you have your own accounts?" as though it were some kind of sin. When I related the federal tax advantages to having my own assets in my own name, he said, "You are absolutely right!" as though it were impossible for a woman to be able to grasp such information. This man was a Trenton lawyer who had been recommended to my husband as one who was a "real tiger" in a divorce action and who would "get everything you are entitled to." He was accustomed to dealing with women who had no knowledge of money and no money of their own. He simply thought he would be able to bulldoze through me and intimidate me.

Handling my own money for years had given me knowledge *and the self confidence* that made me a stronger adversary in this divorce. At the time I earned more money at my job than my husband earned at his job, and I could prove through my own canceled checks that I had paid for major portions of the real estate and other household assets. They were mine because I had earned them, and *I had paid for them.*

Women *earn* a share of the household assets, even if they stay home and do not hold an outside job, but they cannot prove that they have *paid* for their share of the assets unless they have their own income and their own checking accounts. This is an important distinction. Men tend to think that women's work is not valuable. My last husband told his lawyer that all I did was "sit around and do needlepoint." He ignored the fact that I got up a half hour early every morning to make his breakfasts and lunches. He ignored the housekeeping, the entertaining. He paid no attention to the vegetable garden I planted every year, the quarts of peaches I canned every fall. My work simply disappeared from his mind. He discounted the dog work I did on the rental properties: hauling lath and plaster to the dumpsters, peeling off old wallpaper, cleaning up all the trash. Because he did the plumbing and heating installations, he thought he was the only one "working" and therefore he was entitled to the bulk of the assets of the marriage.

For these reasons, what a woman has earned in the marriage is subject to interpretation. The courts must make a judgment about what a woman has been "worth " in the marriage versus what the man has been "worth" in the marriage. In this situation, she often comes off a loser against her husband's paper proof through his pay stubs and canceled checks of what he has earned and what he has paid.

The husband can intimidate his wife on this issue, as mine tried to do to me. I had a friend once, so lacking in self confidence, that when her husband proposed a divorce settlement which consisted of these "concessions" -- that she could live in the house until the kids were raised, but then she had to sell it and give half to him -- that she accepted this and thought it was fair. I sat with her and convinced her that she had earned every penny in that house by staying at home to raise three children for fifteen years. She had no obligation to give her husband a damn thing. As a caring and hard working housewife, she had earned the *entire* value of that house, which at that time might have been worth $70,000. Even then, $70,000 (the equity value of the house) for 15 years of labor is pitiful wages:

<u>CALCULATION:</u> $70,000 divided by 15 years = $4,666 per year.

She subsequently hired her own lawyer and worked diligently to get a good share of the marital assets, despite the fact that her husband had stolen and hidden their tax returns from her, had made over the title to his boat and cars to his brother, and had made every attempt to conceal the amount of money he earned at his printing business.

When you have joint bank accounts, the other person can take the money and run. I have a male friend whose wife did just that. He kept depositing his substantial paychecks into their joint checking account. He didn't keep track of the balances on his monthly statements. He sat back and "trusted" his wife. When his wife left him, unexpectedly, he learned, to his dismay, that he didn't have a dime in his account.

If you have stocks and bonds in joint names, your spouse can request that these securities be sold without your permission. To avert this, you would have to notify your broker not to sell any jointly held securities without your written permission.

You may think that you are happily married and that nothing like this will ever happen to you. I once knew a man who taught at a major university in Washington, D.C. three days a week. He took the train down on a Tuesday and came back on Friday nights to his home in Princeton. He considered himself blissfully happy, no problem in that marriage. Oh, they had their little disagreements, but nothing major.

One Friday night he arrived home to find their huge two story house completely empty except for his own study. He confided to me that he nearly lost his mind. The neighbors told him that two moving vans had arrived that day and cleaned the place out. I know another man who said that his wife did the same thing. When he got home from work, he couldn't even find a can opener. She had only left his squash racquet and his clothes.

Men may not clean out the house when they leave, but they will clean out the financial assets. Since they can prove the value of their labor--they have pay stubs, tax returns, and canceled checks--they are automatically in a position of greater power in a divorce proceeding when it comes to dividing up the family assets.

I hope I have convinced you by the stories above that you need your own bank accounts in your own name. You need your own credit cards in your name. If you work outside the home, you should put your paychecks, or at least a major portion of them, into your own private bank accounts.

If you are married and do not work outside the home, how do you get money of your own? You squirrel it away from the household money you receive from your husband. You take odd part-time jobs. Before you get married, you have your own checking and savings accounts and after you are married, you keep them. Instead of useless

Christmas presents from your parents or family, you ask for money, and you keep it to yourself. If your children receive money as presents, put it into their own private accounts over which you have signatory power

I recently saw a magazine article about hidden bank accounts. This article scolded women for hiding money from their husbands. The article urged the wives to "work things out" with their husbands. This is all very nice if your husband is a giving person, but women would not hide money in the first place if they really trusted their husbands. What I am urging is whether you trust him or not, the power politics of the real world *demand* that you hold control over your own financial assets.

If you have separate accounts, how do you handle the finances? Work it out. I usually paid for all the household food, the furnishings, interior decoration, gardening supplies. My husband usually paid for the cars, the heavy equipment like the refrigerators and stoves. I bought the amenities, the pretty things that gave the house its charm and pleasure. He bought the practicals: the lawn mowers, the garbage cans. We did keep a separate account for all the rental properties. You may wish to have a joint account for a child's education, or to make the house payments if the house is jointly held.

Do what works. But keep some serious amount of money as your own. Keep track of your husband's money via your tax returns. It's insurance in case you are divorced or widowed. You wouldn't want to be without health or life insurance would you? Why should you go without financial insurance?

When you decide what assets to hold jointly, and what assets to hold as your own, you need to understand tax law and probate law. You should consult a good lawyer to decide what kind of ownership best suits your needs; there are several types of **title**. You need to have a written will. When you hold assets jointly with rights of survivorship, it means that if the other person dies before you do, the asset passes directly to you without going through probate. However, as a rule major assets held jointly with rights of survivorship cannot be sold without permission of both partners.

A second form of ownership--tenancy by the entirety--is similar to joint tenancy, but this form of ownership is available in only thirty states, so you need to check it out with a lawyer in your state.

Tenancy in common is a form of ownership were each partner can dispose of his/her share independently. When one owner dies, his share goes to heirs named in a will; it does not automatically pass to the other owners.

Nine states are community property states (Arizona, California, Idaho, Louisiana, Nevada, New Mexico, Texas, Washington, and Wisconsin). The laws regarding property say that both partners own whatever is acquired during the marriage regardless of whose name is on the asset.

There are major tax consequences of various types of ownership. Depending on which type of ownership you choose, you can end up paying more or fewer estate taxes. You need a good tax accountant to help advise you on this issue.

Cars should *never* be held jointly because of the liability involved. If the car is held by two people, both people are responsible for damages in a lawsuit. If the car is held in only one person's name, only that person and his/her assets are vulnerable to a lawsuit. If you have a teenage driver in the house, that child should have the car in his/her own name and be insured in his/her own name, so that in case of major accidents, you will not lose your house or other assets in a lawsuit.

In summary, there are financial and legal reasons for keeping title to bank accounts, credit cards, cars, and in some cases, houses in your name individually separate from the man in your life. There are also important psychological reasons. Knowing that you can do what you wish, that you have financial independence and freedom, bolsters your own self confidence and makes you a more powerful person in this society. Women's shelters have been established because so many women in abusive relationships have no where to go because they have no money of their own. Money is power. You need to have your own power.

CHAPTER TEN: FOUR LIFELONG FINANCIAL DECISIONS

Throughout this book, we've been discussing how to manage money, but we have also been talking about values and choices. How you *choose* to spend your money results from your values: what you think is important in life. I have tried to persuade you to examine your choices and to become aware of the values that underlie your choices. I have urged you to jettison choices that are based on trying to impress other people, that are based on issues of status and prestige rather than sound economics. I have tried to induce you to be aware that much of what you have learned as a woman about handling money is a *myth* that will keep you poor for your lifetime.

Whether you have money or do not have money results from choices you have made during your life, and these choices began very early, starting with whether you finished high school or not. However, few choices are irrevocable, but at this stage of your life, you may think that you have no choices left, that since you don't have much money, you are locked into your present situation. If you believe this, you are defeated instantly. Even now with every purchase you make, you are choosing among different items. There are smart choices and stupid choices facing you, but there are always choices. The trick is to *think* about your choices, and to make wise choices. This will take courage and self discipline. You may have to fight your husband, your boyfriend, your children in order to make the right financial choices. This is not easy work. Nonetheless, the first step in sound money management is to make *conscious, wise* choices. That means, controlling your emotions.

Don't be afraid of making choices. If you do something that you don't like, you can change your mind, and you should feel free to change your mind when you see that a decision you have made is not working for you. You need to feel free to experiment, to find out what works best for you. Throughout this book, I have told you about all the financial mistakes I've made during my life, including bad purchases of furniture and clothing and two poor marriages, so don't be embarrassed. Don't feel that you are alone.

Nonetheless, there are four choices, *emotional choices* a woman can make that narrow all subsequent freedom of financial decision making, choices that can hem her in financially for a lifetime.

The four most expensive financial decisions a woman can make are:

CHOICE # 1: TO HAVE CHILDREN

Each woman must make this decision for herself. I only wish to emphasize that when you have children, you have chosen to siphon off thousands of dollars to the care and support of those children, money that you could use for other purposes. The decision to have children is a financial decision as well as a personal or psychological decision.

The problem with having children is that in the first two years of their lives, they are relatively inexpensive to have. If you are covered with medical insurance that pays for the birth, the pre-natal care, you may not think that having a baby is costly. But when that child begins growing, your expenses will escalate and continue to increase until that child leaves home.

The expense of children increases in direct proportion to the kind of future you want for that child or those children. Do you want them to be in vigorous health? This costs money for medication, doctor visits, and nutritious food. It may also involve special classes in various kinds of athletics to insure strong physical development, or special tutoring to compensate for some sort of disability.

Do you want those children to be highly educated so they can get good jobs and participate fully in the demands of this complex society? This costs money for books, personal computers, perhaps extra tutoring, college tuition. At the present time, costs for room, board and tuition at a public college average about $5,000 per year. Room, board and tuition at a private college average about $13,000 per year. Yet a college education almost always assures a higher income throughout one's life, as I discussed earlier in this book. In 1991, the average hourly wage paid to high school dropouts was $7.62. The average hourly wage paid to a high school graduate was $9.43. College graduates averaged $14.77 an hour, while those with postgraduate work or graduate degrees to their credit averaged $19.24 an hour. (Source: "*Business Week* 1992 Special Bonus Issue).

Do you want your children to experience life's amenities so that they can be comfortable in all kinds of society--amenities such as travel, restaurant meals, visits to museums, concerts, art galleries? This costs money. The more children you have, the higher your housing costs, your food costs, your clothing and medical costs, even before getting to education and amenities.

Raising your children will often prevent you from leading your own life. You want to write? You want a better job? You want to go back to school, get a college degree? You want to travel? When women have children, they usually forfeit these kinds of fulfillment until the children are grown. The expenses of their children may eliminate all of these luxuries for mothers for their entire lives. I know women here, where I live, who had four children, and who now live a rather circumscribed life because of the money they spent raising their children. This doesn't mean that they don't love their children. It simply means that children take money and time away from your life to the extent that by the time they've left home, you may have very little time and money remaining of your own.

Women postpone major portions of their lives for at least twenty years or more when they have children. I know of women who impulsively decided that they "loved" children and had three or four within the first years of their young adult lives. Then reality arrived. Their lives revolve around children. They love their children, but few women have no other ambition than to raise children. I know women who now work in low level, boring jobs, who struggle to take singing lessons, to study art, to write, while juggling large families and strained finances. Their discontent and frustration begins to tarnish their love for their children and their husbands.

Recently I watched a program on TV about parents going back to finish high school at the same high school where their children are enrolled. These parents gave birth to these children when they were 12, 13, 14 years old. They dropped out of school, but now they realize what they lost, and they are trying to recapture those lost opportunities.

You may be happily married now. What happens if you are divorced? What happens if your husband dies early or is disabled? Then the support of your children may fall entirely upon your shoulders, and thus far, the U.S. Government does little to help women in this position. Can you handle this kind of financial burden? Think about it.

DECISION#2. TO GET DIVORCED OR REMAIN UNMARRIED.

Married couples and their households are richer than are households headed by unmarried adults. This greater wealth for married households occurs primarily for two reasons. First, men earn more money than women, even when they hold the same jobs as women. Second, joint households create "**economies of scale.**" That is, two people living in one house save money compared with two people living separately in two houses or apartments. When purchasing groceries, you can buy in larger, cheaper quantities to feed larger households. The cost of heating one house to warm an entire family is lower than heating two houses to warm two people or two families. These are "**economies of scale.**"

If you are presently married, only you can judge the trade-offs between the greater financial comfort of being married and the advantages of getting divorced and living alone. I certainly do not urge you to remain in an unhappy marriage just for money, but among other things, getting a divorce is a major financial decision. If you have the training and education that will allow you to hold a good paying job, then the decision will be easier.

I have a friend who has suffered from several bouts of cancer. She remains in an unhappy marriage because of her husband's health insurance, which covers her medical care. If she divorces him, she will not have insured medical care.

If you are in a difficult relationship with a man, and you do not have the necessary job skills to support yourself adequately, use your husband's money to go back to school to learn a skill that will give you financial freedom. You are entitled to do this.

I know a woman who wanted to get divorced. Before she did, she managed to persuade her husband to finance her efforts to obtain a B.A. degree from Brooklyn College. He objected. He said, "Why don't you just go back to being an X-ray technician like you did before we were married?" She flatly refused. As an X-ray technician she would never earn enough money to live comfortably, since it only paid about $7 an hour at that time. She could not possibly maintain the same standard of living on that salary that she had while married. On the other hand, living with her husband had become intolerable. Fortunately, she was able to negotiate with him to pay for her further education, and despite raising three children at the time, she went on to obtain her masters degree in art history and Chinese art, and she has a new job as a museum director in the city where she lives. This is a far, far cry from being slotted into the boredom of an X-ray technician. No one supported this woman in her efforts. Her family criticized her. Her husband pressured her. No one wanted her to become independent and accomplished. They wanted her to remain the little Irish girl, dutiful to family, that she had always been. She refused and has no regrets.

Whether you are happily or unhappily married, do not have any qualms about getting your husband to finance your further education. As discussed earlier, people with a college degree generally earn nearly double what a high school graduate earns. However, you must allow for the fact that regardless of education, women tend to earn only about 69% of what men in the same job earn. (Source: "*Business Week* 1992 Special Bonus Issue.") So even if you do have a college degree, your standard of living will likely be less as a single woman than that of a single man.

Even if you are happily married, I urge you to gain as much education as possible. It will broaden your life, lead to greater happiness, and if you are widowed, it will help you support yourself if you must.

Living as a single woman is not easy, especially if you have children to raise. However, sooner or later, almost all women will be single. A married woman has a 70% chance of outliving her husband, of living her final years as a widow. One in two marriages ends in divorce. You need to prepare yourself to live alone by learning how to manage your money and your own happiness.

DECISION# 3. TO LEND MONEY TO A HUSBAND, LOVER, FRIEND.

Lending money to anyone is pure gambling. It means you have money to burn. Your chances of ever being repaid are remote.

There is a saying that if it "walks like a duck, quacks like a duck, and looks like a duck, it's a duck." This means that a person's *behavior* is the surest indicator of what kind of person he/she is. If a man needs to borrow money from you, it means he doesn't know how to handle money. If he knew how to handle money, he wouldn't need to borrow from you. It's that simple, and a woman ignores this at her peril.

Let's discuss lending money to a friend or lover.

Women lend money to their lovers because they love them and they want to help them. Women give out of love, but I have never encountered a man who pays back a loan out of love. No matter how often a man says he will pay you back, you will be extremely lucky if he does. Men are often great liars. When dealing with women, they are taught to lie from the time they are young men. They are taught to tell a woman that they love her when in fact all they want to do is to sleep with her. And since women often believe these lies, men continue to lie. It works for them.

If you have lent money to your lover, you will often be forced to maintain the relationship just to try to get your money back. This is degrading. I know of a woman who is in precisely this position. She no longer loves the man; she would like to get him out of her life, but he owes her so much money she cannot afford to abandon the relationship.

I know another woman who lent a man $10,000 to pay the property taxes on his house, which he had let fall into arrears. His wife had left him, and she had served him with divorce papers. This man assured his lover he would pay her back as soon as the house was sold. Then his wife changed her mind about the divorce and moved back in with him. Needless to say, he did not pursue the divorce, nor did he pay off the $10,000 he owed.

He now had the money to do so. His wife worked and brought in an excellent salary. The two of them proceeded to redecorate their house with new wall-to-wall carpeting, new draperies, a remodeled kitchen and bathroom. He leased a new BMW car for himself, and his wife bought an Audi, but he still paid nothing of the $10,000 he owed the other woman, his so-called "lover." He offered many excuses, but finally this woman cut off the relationship, and they were no longer lovers. Nonetheless, she kept after him for the money he owed her. Fortunately, she had made him sign an IOU for the money. He had made a few small payments on the loan, and she had kept a written record of them. After five years of waiting, she threatened to take him to court to get the money from him. He was well respected in the community with a reputation to lose. He didn't want his wife to know about this loan or about his love affair. He finally paid the principal, but he never paid the interest he owed his former lover.

If you insist on lending money to a lover, obtain an IOU from him, a contract showing that he owes you the money and the terms under which he is to repay it. If he doesn't repay, take him to court. Publicity is a great cure for obtaining repayment of debts. Many men have illicit affairs while they are married and holding down responsible positions at work. Threatening a court action brings this covert life into the open. Most men cannot tolerate that possibility, but it means you have to be very tough.

Nonetheless, the key thing to remember is that if the man in your life cannot borrow money from the bank, it means he is a bad risk. If a bank will not lend to him, why should you? You can afford to lose the money even less than a bank can afford to. The reason people do not have the money they need is usually because they have managed it poorly to begin with.

The man described above did not have the money he needed because he spent his money foolishly. Whenever he was at a party in a restaurant or bar, he insisted on buying everyone's drinks. He bought expensive cars and drove them excessively because he didn't want to bother taking public transportation. He bought expensive clothes. He bought a costly, "classic" car for his son and then paid for all the repairs on it. He did not insist that his son pay for the car or its upkeep. Most seriously, he failed to file his income tax returns, so the Internal

Revenue Service hit him for enormous fines and penalties. This man was college educated. He had no excuse for not knowing the IRS rules regarding the filing of tax returns, but he was too lazy and self indulgent to spend the time learning. He was too arrogant to believe that he needed the advice of a tax accountant.

This man did not bother to open his mail regularly. As a consequence he failed to file for homestead tax rebates for three years, which would have brought him about $500 in tax refunds. These behaviors all indicate poor money management skills. That's why this man needed to borrow money. That's why his lover should never have lent it to him regardless of how much she cared for him originally.

It is always hard to judge a person. Are they reliable or not? Are they honest? Many people get into financial difficulties because they lend to people they think they can trust. Only when it is too late do they learn that the person they trusted is a scoundrel, or at best simply stupid about handling money. Your only protection in such a case is to say to yourself, "If the bank will not lend this person money, then he must be a bad risk. Can I afford to throw money away on a bad risk if a bank cannot?" You must not let your love for this person enter into it. This sounds harsh, but it is absolutely essential to your own security to think of yourself first, rather than your lover.

When a person borrows money and does not pay it back, it is theft, plain and simple. Your lover is a robber if he does not pay you back. He is a cheat and a liar. The man described above spent money to maintain his image as a successful, generous person, when in fact he was stealing money from the woman who had lent it to him. Of course he did not see himself as a thief. He just never "had the money" to pay her back. He kept promising to pay her, but he did not do it until she threatened to take him to court.

When it comes to money, talk is cheap. Do not pay any attention to what your lover tells you about how he "needs" the money, how he will pay you back "soon." Look at the facts. Is he curtailing his own lifestyle to save money? Is he sacrificing his own personal comfort in order to get the money to repay you? If not, take him to court as quickly as possible.

Lending Money to Your Husband

What do I mean by "lending money" to your husband? A woman lends or gives money to her husband when she doesn't know what he is doing with her (their) money. A woman gambles with her life if she lets her husband handle all the money of the household without knowing *exactly* what he is doing with it. By her ignorance, she lends money to her husband by default.

Women feel that to suspect a husband's motives with regard to how he handles her money (or the household money) means that she does not love him or does not "trust" him. This is nonsense. This is misguided love and misguided trust. If your husband is worthy of your love and trust, he will be delighted to share his financial management decisions with you. He will explain precisely what he is doing with the money to help you understand so that in the event that he dies or is disabled, you will be able to care for yourself. A man who is not willing to do this wants you to be in his power, to be his victim. Such a man does not love you. He simply owns you, and you cannot allow this for your own self respect and your own security in the event you are left alone through death or divorce.

You may think that your husband's willingness to handle all the finances, to keep you from worrying about money, is a sign of his care for you. Do not delude yourself. This kind of care keeps you completely dependent on your husband. He has the power over you. Maybe it is a benign power, but it is extremely dangerous for your own welfare to be this dependent.

Recently I read of woman, happily married, who knew nothing about how her husband handled their money until she learned that he had rashly speculated in the stock market with all of their retirement money. He had lost $180,000. At age 65, she was forced to return to work She had, through her ignorance, given her share of the family's money to her husband, no questions asked, and he had lost it. Now they were both nearly bankrupt, but she, being the younger, was the one who had to go back to work.

I recently read a pitiful story about a woman who got divorced and in exchange for money paid by his wife to him for his share of their home, her husband agreed to pay taxes on income he had not declared in two previous years. She didn't know he had cheated the Internal Revenue Service when she signed their joint returns. He subsequently filed for bankruptcy and did not pay the back taxes he owed. Since she had the only family assets--their home--the IRS told her that she was now liable for her former husband's $70,000 in back taxes, fines, and interest charges. The IRS has put a lien on her house. She now must pay all of this money. Her future is in hock for years and years because she did not pay attention to her husband's financial dealings, and she signed their joint tax returns in total ignorance of what they contained, or in this case, did not contain.

Do not ever sign a joint tax return with your husband unless you know absolutely that it is an honest return or you can be held liable for back taxes and penalties.

DECISION #4: TO BUY "INTO" THE AMERICAN MARKET ECONOMY.

The American economy thrives on training women to "shop until they drop." The advice you receive in women's magazines, newspapers, and on television concentrates on "shopping." You are urged to comparison shop, to shop for bargains, to check prices, to buy name brands, to buy "quality", to buy "image", to buy "prestige," to buy "status." The worst part about this shopping mentality is that women "buy" into the notion that their happiness depends on looking beautiful and spending money to do this.

I am the last person to say that being attractive is not rewarding, but your attractiveness depends on who you are, not how much money you have spent on your appearance. Whether you are attractive or not can cost you practically nothing because true attractiveness depends on your spirit, your optimism, your comfort inside your skin, your contentment with the life you have chosen for yourself. It depends on your own excitement and joy in life and the people around you, and not on the clothes on your back.

I know a woman who has recently had two face lifts to improve her appearance. None of her friends or acquaintances can see any significant difference in how she looks, and her looks are not good. Her hair is bleached to the point where it has no shine. She wears such long false finger nails she can hardly type, and thus she takes longer to do her work than she should. She smokes incessantly, so her skin is getting wrinkled, and she smells like a dirty ashtray whenever you are near her. She could have face lifts from now until doomsday and she would not be any more attractive.

Yet I have known women, with little money, who are immensely over weight but who give off charm and delight because of their sense of humor and their enthusiasm for life. A sour disposition and cigarettes will ruin your charm more than anything you are wearing.

When you "buy" into the American shopping ethic, you are told that comparison shopping will "save you money." As I've tried to demonstrate in earlier chapters, this is one of the greatest myths in America. With rare exceptions comparison shopping is a serious waste of time. It may be fun to shop, but you will not save significant amounts of money by shopping. Although advertisements may stress "saving money", what they really say is "buy, buy, buy." If you keep buying, you will remain poor.

Believe me, merchandisers are not in business to *save you money.* They are in business to *earn money for themselves.* They are clever. They spend millions of dollars on advertising and methods of stacking the shelves in their stores so you will buy, buy, and buy some more, whether you need it or not.

It seems obvious, but one of the best ways to hang on to your money is not to buy things with it.

I have been sucked into the American "buy" economy as often as anyone. Even now, I find myself envying my neighbors. They have built a beautiful new house full of lovely "things." Oil burning candles on the coffee tables; beautiful original watercolor paintings on the walls, balloon window hangings in gorgeous chintz prints, thick wall to wall carpeting throughout the house.

I come back to my house with its bare windows, it's ugly brown carpet worn and torn in spots, and I want to run right out to the stores and buy things to make my house as lovely.

Right now, I cannot afford to do this. And in my heart of hearts I know that whether I decorate my house differently or not will have absolutely no impact on who my friends are and it will not affect my overall happiness significantly.

You can choose to spend money on *who you are*. That is, you can spend money on your brain or your talents--lessons in art or music, books, concerts--activities that broaden your outlook, enrich your spirit, that make you an interesting person to be with.

You can choose to spend money on *things*. You can buy and furnish a fine home. You can buy cars. You can buy fur coats, fancy clothes, a new pair of shoes with every dress, bathroom soaps, cosmetics.

You can choose to spend money on *activities*. You can take long vacations to exotic places. You can play tennis, golf, and go skiing. You can spend money on an active life going to concerts or plays, going out to restaurants and sports events.

You can spend money on the *people* in your life: your children, your other family members or friends.

You can spend a little money in each of the categories above. Wherever you spend your money, it is your choice, and it's an *emotional* decision as well as a *financial* decision.

SECTION FOUR: BASIC FINANCIAL PLANNING

ELEVEN: BUDGETS

Budgets guide your spending. They fence in your impulse to spend money that you don't have. They can prevent your spending money on things that you don't need. Budgets act like signposts on highways: they tell you where you are and where you are going before you get there. They keep you on the right road to meeting your financial goals. Budgets will only work, however, if you discipline yourself to use them and follow them. It does no good to have a budget and then ignore it.

When people are trying to gain control over their spending, financial advisors and counselors recommend that they keep track of nearly every penny they spend, a time consuming procedure. Keeping these kinds of records allows a person or family to actually see its priorities. For example, if after two or three months of keeping such records, you learn that you spend $200 a month on eating meals out and only $25 a month goes toward a college education fund for your children, you know that your priorities focus on immediate pleasure at the expense of your children's future.

Thus, the first step in setting up a household budget is to itemize your present spending habits. You must know roughly where you spend your money now. If you think it would be helpful to keep track of every penny you spend, or at least every dollar, for a month or two in order to document where you actually spend your money, by all means do so. On the other hand, you can go through your canceled checks and the statements from your charge accounts and get fairly accurate estimates of where you spend you money each month. Whether you list every penny or give fairly close estimates of actual expenditures, list your expenses on a large yellow lined tablet or piece of paper in the categories shown below. Set up categories as follows:

Utilities
- Electric
- Gas, propane, firewood
- Telephone
- Cellular phone, car phone
- Water
- Garbage collection

Food
- Food in home
- Restaurant meals, outside the home meals

Charge Accounts
- Clothing
- Household
- Lawn, garden, yard care

Mortgage Payments
- Home equity loan payments

Insurance
- Auto
- Homeowners
- Health
- Life
- Disability
- Other insurance (umbrella liability)

Medical, dental, other health care (vitamins)

Charitable contributions, church pledges

Entertainment (movies, theater, VCR tape rentals, concerts, dances)
- Monthly cable TV
- Magazine, newspaper subscriptions, book purchases, library cards

Car expenses
- Gasoline, oil
- Repairs, maintenance, tires

Taxes
- Property taxes
- Other taxes, home owner association dues

Savings, investments

You may have other categories to add to these. When you have listed all your expenses for a year, add them up. They should come to nearly what you took home in pay for the year. If your take home pay is $400 a week, x 52 weeks = $20,800, your records of expenses and bills paid should come to within $20,000. If you cannot account for at least 90% of all the money you spent during the past year, you are carrying a lot of cash which you are spending randomly. If your numbers show that you have spent more than you earned, you are digging your way into serious debt.

An important part of controlling your finances is to keep only *small* amounts of cash on hand. Cash disappears like air. When you have cash in your wallet, it is easier to treat people to drinks after work at the local bar. It is easier to buy food from the vending machines at work. If you go shopping on your lunch hour, it is easier to spend the cash on some impulse buying. Somehow, it is harder, at least psychologically, to spend money using a credit card or a check rather than using cash. More importantly, your credit card bills and your canceled checks allow you to keep close records of how you've spent your money, which using cash will not do.

After you have a pretty good idea of where your money has gone during the past year, you can set up a realistic budget for yourself. You will know what **fixed costs** you must meet each month--rent or mortgage, car payments, etc. You will also be able to move your spending from one category to another, cutting down on entertainment for example, and increasing your savings.

To begin budgeting, on the first day of every month on a big pad of yellow lined paper, list the same spending categories you used to determine where you spent your money during the past year. List them down the side of the yellow tablet. Beside each category, insert the *estimated* amount of money you think you will spend in that category during the coming month.

In some categories, you will know exactly how much money you will spend because they are **fixed expenses** that do not vary from month to month. For some categories, you can write in a rough estimate of what you spend based on past experience, or you can write in what you think is a *reasonable or a smart* amount to spend each month. For those expenses that you pay every three months, divide the total amount by 3 to get your monthly payment. Your monthly budget should look approximately like this:

Spending Category	Estimated Amount
Mortgage or rent payment	$500.00
Car payment	$135.00
Escrow for property taxes	$100.00
Television cable bill	$20.00
Monthly insurance payments	$100.00
Electric bill	$35.00
Gas bill	$80.00
Telephone bill	$50.00
Food at $125 per week, 4 weeks	$500.00
MasterCard/Visa bill, other charge cards	$200.00
Entertainment (video rentals, movies)	$100.00
Savings (for emergencies, insurance payments, etc.)	$100.00
TOTAL ESTIMATED MONTHLY EXPENSES	$1920.00

I usually include my gasoline, postage, drugstore, liquor, and other small items in my monthly food budget so I don't have too many categories of expenses. I cash a check at the supermarket each week for $125 and out of that I not only buy my food, but pay for those miscellaneous expenses. This is the only amount of cash that I usually allow myself. All other purchases are made with credit cards or checks. If you have other categories than those I've listed above, add them to your budget.

The figures I have inserted above may or may not reflect your actual spending patterns. I have used them to give you an idea of how to set up a budget. You should insert your own numbers for your budget.

Notice that I have inserted *savings* as part of your budget. One of the biggest mistakes that people make in handling their finances is not to set aside a specific amount for savings each month. It is this build up of savings that allows you to pay in full for that new washing machine rather than renting to own or paying for it over a period of months. Having cash savings allows you to pay for your insurance when it comes due. Today I just paid my cable bill for the entire year, thus saving myself $38 over what it would cost me to pay the bill each month.

The best way to handle your savings is to put it aside, into a bank savings account, at the *beginning* of each month. Even if they try to save, people usually leave savings for the end of the month, as some sort of leftover after everything else has been bought. Then, they overspend and are never able to set the money aside. Think of your savings as essential, like food and rent. It is.

Now, compare your estimated expenses for the month with your **after tax** income for the month. Remember, after tax income is the money from any paychecks you receive after all of the income tax, social security and other withholding have been deducted. It's your take home pay. If you are paid by the week, multiply your take home pay by four weeks in the month. Write that amount at the bottom of your tablet, next to your estimated monthly expenses.

For our hypothetical person, let's assume that she earns $10 an hour for a 40 hour week, and her gross income for a month will be about $1600. After deductions, (I will subtract $350, which is about what social security and federal income tax withholding would be), her monthly income, **after tax**, is only $1250.

In the budget shown above, if you subtract this amount from the estimated monthly expenses, you can see that this person is in trouble financially. In the example above, she has a **deficit** of $670; that is, her estimated monthly expenses are greater than her monthly income by $670 for that month.

If you are running a deficit, you are living beyond your income. You are spending more than you earn. A budget lets you know this each month so you can begin to cut back on your spending before you get into serious financial trouble. There is only one way to get out of this kind of situation: get tough on yourself.

Where to begin? A person can only cut back on those expenses which are not **fixed** each month. Rent and car payments are **fixed** expenses over which one has relatively little control. It is very important to keep your **fixed** expenses as low as possible because they are hard to change. The only way you can alter monthly car expenses is to drive your car long enough so that you do not have car payments.

The only way you can alter your fixed housing costs is to stay in an old house or a small apartment as long as possible rather than moving to a newer, more expensive home. If your income increases, but your housing costs remain constant or go up more slowly than your income, then you create more **disposable** or flexible income for yourself.

When you think about buying a house, figure out your mortgage payments on a monthly basis, as part of your total budget to see whether you can really afford to buy that house. Remember to add in the property taxes you will pay. Similarly, when you rent. Try to rent an apartment as cheaply as possible to keep your monthly payments as low as possible.

In the past, experts have recommended that your mortgage or rent should amount to only 25% - 33% of your monthly income. These figures have crept upward, but they are an excellent guidepost to follow when making a decision about buying or renting a specific home. Paying money for deluxe shelter when moderate shelter will do is a common way that people get into financial difficulties. Try not to upgrade your housing until you have substantial money saved for emergencies and for other investments.

Since **fixed costs** cannot easily be changed, the only way to manage a financial **deficit** like the one in the budget above is to cut small amounts where possible from each category, and eliminate those items which are not absolutely necessary. I would start by disconnecting the cable TV service. I would eliminate entertainment or cut it down to about $25 a month. I would cut another $25 a week off the food and miscellaneous budget. (If you smoke, you can probably save this much money by quitting smoking.) Definitely cut out all liquor consumption. Cut back on your driving to lower the amount you spend for gas each week. Cut back on your consumption of convenience foods and make your own, as I've discussed earlier. I would try not to charge more than $100 a month on my credit cards. I would lower my savings budget to $25 a month. I would cut back my telephone calls to lower that bill to $30 a month. If possible, simply disconnect the phone. If you have to go to a pay phone every time you make a telephone call, your phone bill will drop drastically. It's inconvenient, but it can be done. I would try to lower my heating and air conditioning costs so that my gas bill falls to $60 a month. Keep your rooms at 55 - 60 degrees at night. Use an electric blanket instead of heating the house. Keep a blanket across your knees when you sit at night. Wear sweaters. During summers, use fans instead of air conditioning. If you must use air conditioning, set it so that it starts at 80 degrees rather than 70 degrees.

I would try to lower that electric bill to $30 by turning off the TV as much as possible. Many people turn the TV on like a radio, and keep it on all day whether they watch it or not. This wastes money and wears out your TV so you will have to buy a new one sooner. Also, the dishwasher consumes a lot of electricity. Wash dishes by hand.

The basic principle outlined above is to make many small cuts rather than one huge cut. Many small cuts are often the only way to balance one's budget. Now, let's see where these cuts have taken us.

Mortgage or rent payment	$500.00
Car payment	$135.00
Escrow for property taxes	$100.00
Electric bill	$30.00
Gas bill	$60.00
Telephone bill	$30.00
Food at $100 per week, 4 weeks	$400.00
Television cable bill	none
Charge card bills	$100.00
Entertainment (video rentals, dinners out)	$25.00
Savings (for emergencies, insurance payments, etc.)	$25.00
TOTAL ESTIMATED EXPENSES	$1475.00

This woman is still $225 short for the month. Her only alternative is to cut out all entertainment, her savings, and any charges on her credit cards. She may also be able to find someone to share her home or apartment and split the rent or mortgage payments. If she does this, remember that rent money is income that is taxable by the federal income tax. This woman may get someone to share rides with her in her car and share part of the expenses, or she could try to share rides with someone else, leaving her car at home for a few days each month.

You now see how a budget can work for you. If you have constantly, each month, written out your *actual* expenses as well as your *estimated* expenses, and compared them to your **after tax** income, you will know when your spending has gone beyond your income before it is too late. You will know when you cannot afford to make another purchase because you will not be able to pay for it during the next month. The monthly budget tells you immediately when you are in financial difficulty and how serious the problem is. It can also tell you when you are doing well financially, when you have extra money which you can and *should* immediately stash into your savings account.

As each bill comes in during the month, pay it and cross it off your list. Make a new list, adding up your remaining estimated costs compared with your remaining estimated income. Keep the two numbers in balance. If you have less income than expected bills, try to cut some of the remaining expenses. If you have more income than estimated expenses, put that extra money immediately into your savings account.

The underlying assumption behind the budget process I have shown you is that you will live on a *month-to-month* basis, and that in every month, your expenses will not exceed your income. This takes discipline and hard work.

I cannot emphasize enough the need to live **month to month.** You may think that well, this month my expenses are more than my income, but I can make it up next month. Occasionally, this is necessary, but if you continue to do this month after month, at the end of a year, you will have spent more than you have earned.

People who run deficits in their budgets month after month, who keep extending their expenses further into the future without balancing their budgets, go deeper into debt and can ultimately go bankrupt. They are like our federal government.

You will notice that I have always budgeted on a four week monthly budget, but that in any given year, four months will have five weeks of pay days (if you get paid weekly). These four extra pay weeks give you four extra weeks of *padding* or emergency cushion. Try never to calculate these four weeks into your monthly budget. If possible, when this extra week of pay arrives, put it into your savings account, or pay off any revolving charge account balances that you have, or make a larger mortgage payment.

Keeping a budget is simple and should become absolutely routine for you. A budget is a working tool, not something set in concrete. It provides guidelines and data that enable you to adjust your spending patterns. Budgets will tell you when you should look for a new job to earn more money, or when to look for a new job to cut down on such expenses as commuting costs. Budgets will show you where you can cut, and where it is impossible to cut. Budgets will show you that you cannot spend $500 on Christmas presents this year because you will never be able to make up that deficit during the coming months.

I have emphasized more than once in this book that getting rich takes self discipline. Following a budget is where the discipline counts. Use any surplus money you have to earn more money for yourself by lowering debt and interest charges or by saving it to become **capital** for future investment instead of using surplus money to have a fling or to splurge on a meal out or new clothes as most people do. This type of decision separates out the wise spender from the foolish spender. A lifetime of such decisions makes the difference between remaining poor, or only moderately comfortable, and getting rich, or at least being very comfortable.

I have a friend who has a large family and serious financial difficulties which came upon him suddenly and could not have been anticipated. This man tightened up. At Christmas, he and his wife did not buy gifts for their children. They did not send out Christmas cards.

They did not spend money on lavish food and drink and entertainment during the holidays. They used this period of relative poverty to spend time together, playing games, going for walks, inventing activities to do as a family. He told me that it was "the best Christmas we've ever had. The kids loved it."

Compare this with another family that has routinely spent hundreds of dollars on toys for their kids to have that "special" Christmas, to fulfill that empty "image" of perfect Christmas happiness advertised in the media to encourage rash spending. Within days, the toys are broken or discarded. Family and friends are disenchanted with expensive gifts they cannot use and did not want. People are stuffed and slightly sick from too much rich food and candy. The $500 to $1,000 spent each year on this frivolity, if saved, would go a long way toward providing a college education for their children. Instead, these parents say, "Well, the kids will just have to fend for themselves. We can't afford to send them to college." This is a perfect example of shiftlessness and irresponsibility, sacrificing children's future education in the name of a plastic Christmas.

It takes guts to go against the trends, to say, I cannot afford to spend my time and my money this way, but it is worth it in the long run. It takes courage and determination not to get suckered into the "shopping" and "spending" economy.

For years I have pleaded with people *not* to give me presents, and I have announced up front and early that I do not buy Christmas presents. If I have time, I bake bread to give to people. For very special friends, I'll treat them to a lunch out, or invite them over for a special dinner I've cooked at home. Some years I send cards, some years I don't. It depends on how I feel both psychologically and financially. My parents and I stopped giving gifts years ago because we realized that we could not give anything that either of us needed or wanted. They had the money to buy anything they wanted, and I didn't want them buying me useless gifts that I hated. I have not noticed that I've lost friends or family as a result of this policy. In fact, it makes Christmas happier and more relaxed for all of us.

I knew a woman who, every year, "redecorated" her two daughters' bedrooms. She bought new curtains, matching sheets and comforters, small throw rugs. It was a gift she gave them every summer while they were away at camp. Yet this woman complained constantly about how poor she was. She was a compulsive shopper, and she was teaching her girls to behave the same way. If she had taken the $200 she spent every summer and invested it, little by little she would have accumulated **capital**, which would have allowed her to eliminate her time payments and charge account fees.

Your economic life is a series of small decisions, but in the end, they add up to big money, either lost or saved. The choice is yours.

CHAPTER TWELVE: YOUR NET WORTH

A budget works from month to month to insure that you live within your income. A **net worth** statement comes at the end of the year and will show you whether you have become richer or poorer during the year. Your **net worth** is the amount of money you would hold in your hand if you were to sell everything you own and pay off all of your debts. If after you sold everything and paid off all your debts, you still owed money, you would be in serious financial trouble. You would have a **negative net worth.**

New Year's Day is a good time to prepare your **net worth** statement. The one I will show you below is very simple. It may not include all of the items that a certified financial planner would include, but it will be a good place for you to begin to trace your progress toward greater financial independence.

Get out your large tablet of yellow lined paper. Line it vertically into four columns, as shown and then list the following items in each column. I am going to insert hypothetical numbers in the columns below, but you should put in the numbers that refer to you and your household. Your assets are all property that you own. Your debts or liabilities are the amounts you owe on the property. Some assets you will own free and clear. Some debts, such as credit cards, will not have any assets attached to them.

When estimating your net worth, you may have to guess about the values of your house, your car, your personal belongings. You can estimate the value of your house by reading the real estate advertisements of your local newspaper to see what comparable houses are selling for. Of course, if you have no house of your own, you have no asset there. If you are young, this net worth statement will help you realize the value of trying to buy your own home rather than living in rental apartments.

Asset	Market Value	Liability	Amount
House	$100,000.00	Mortgage	$75,000.00
Car	$15,000.00	Car Loan	$10,000.00
Savings account	$1,000.00		
Cash value-life insurance	$5,000.00	Credit cards	$3,500.00
Furniture, personal property	$10,000.00	College loans	$5,000.00
Investments	$4,000.00		
Total	**$135,000.00**		**$93,500.00**

When you subtract the **liabilities** (debts) from the **assets** in the example above, you find that the net worth for that household is $41,500.

The value of your house will fluctuate, up or down. For example, two years after I bought my former house, it was worth about $375,000 on the current real estate market. I carried this value on my net worth statement. Then, real estate prices dropped substantially. I was able to sell that house for only $305,000. Thus, my estimated net worth had declined during four years by $70,000 because of the drop in housing prices.

If you own any stocks or bonds or other investments, they should be included as assets in your net worth statement. I do not include money in my savings account if I know that I must pay it all out during a month or two for property taxes. I do not include the cash balance in my checking account since I use it to pay my bills monthly.

It really does not matter too much what you decide to include or exclude from your net worth statement as long as you have included the bulk of your salable assets and all of your debts. Each year, use the same basic items in your net worth statement so you can compare your financial progress from year to year. However, if you have managed to accumulate enough cash to buy stocks or mutual funds, of course you will add those into your net worth statement. You should also add any additional debt you may have accumulated, such as college loans, or money you have borrowed in a home equity loan.

If someone owes you money, that is an asset, but only if you have a reasonable assurance that the money will be repaid to you. If you owe someone, your parents for example, that is a legitimate debt and should be included in your net worth statement as a **liability**.

When estimating the value of your property--car, house, home furnishings--be very conservative. Do not estimate a higher value than you could reasonably expect if you sold those items on the open market, perhaps no more than 10 cents for every dollar you spent on the furniture unless the furniture is truly antique, not just old. If you inflate the value of what you own, you lie to yourself, and you hurt only yourself.

By keeping this yearly net worth statement, you will have a continuing picture of how you are managing your finances. The net worth statement shows your progress toward **capital accumulation.**

I have always found it more fun to do my net worth statement on New Year's Day than to do any New Year's Resolutions, especially if I show an increase in my net worth. I enjoy getting richer.

At present I prepare a net worth statement four times a year and a budget every month. I am now retired, and I work closely with my financial advisor to insure that I am not living beyond the level of income he can generate from my investments. I use the net worth statement to monitor the investment decisions of my financial advisor each quarter: are his investment decisions making money for me, or losing money and at what rate.

CHAPTER THIRTEEN: YOUR ACTION PLAN

Let's briefly summarize the material we have covered thus far. First, recognize that every choice you make in your life has financial repercussions, and some of these repercussions will last you a lifetime, such as the decision to have children or to get divorced or married.

Second, you can see that in order to become financially secure in this society, you must undertake a program of **capital accumulation;** that is, you need to save money to invest in assets that will make money for you while you sleep. To accumulate **capital**, you cannot depend entirely on your wages because they are heavily taxed by federal, state and local governments.

Knowing this, where should you begin in your program of **capital accumulation?** The first place is with either your job or your husband's job. If you do not presently have a paying job, you need to figure out whether you can earn more **after tax income** staying at home or going out to work.

You should evaluate a job in terms of:

The salary it pays
The fringe benefits it pays (or does not pay), especially medical costs.
The personal costs to you of holding that job, including transportation, clothing, and commuting time.
The opportunities for professional advancement.
Pension provisions

If after your evaluation, you decide that you should find another job, how do you go about it?

The absolute best way of finding a new job is to have such a good performance record at your present job, that you can ask people you know to recommend you for a new job. You must have a good performance though, or your friends and acquaintances will not stick their necks out to recommend you to a new job or introduce you to people who can offer you a new job. This use of friends, acquaintances, former employers to help you land a job is called **networking.**

In the section on "The Home Office and Record Keeping," I outlined the need to keep the names and addresses of all people who are favorably disposed toward you so that you can call upon them to help you find a new job. Use former teachers to help you or to provide you with recommendations. Keep a list of everyone you have ever helped or worked for or had a close long-term association with so that you can ask these people for their help.

A second way of finding a job is to work for a temporary office help or employment organization for a while. When you work as temp, you have access to a wide variety of companies and organizations. You find out what kind of jobs are out there and what it takes to get them. You meet new people who can provide you with recommendations. You are exposed to a variety of office procedures and other types of work environments. If you work diligently, you will learn new job skills that will make you a valuable employee. You will learn about jobs that are available but which are never advertised in the newspapers. And importantly, if you work well as a temp, you may be offered a permanent job. According to a recent article in *Money* magazine, about 30% of temporary jobs turn into permanent jobs. (September 1993.)

Many years ago, I worked for a temporary office help company. One of my assignments was to work for two weeks in the medical records department of a large hospital. I simply typed all day, but I had never heard of medical records as a profession, and I learned about other types of jobs available in a hospital. While there, I asked my supervisor if I could practice typing on an electric typewriter. She said yes, so whenever I could I went down to another floor to practice typing on an electric typewriter, which I did for two weeks. When I left the hospital, I told my prospective new employer that I was qualified to work on an electric typewriter, and I found a full time job, through a friend of my husband, as a portfolio typist with, a large investment banking firm. The wages and benefits were far superior to anything I could have earned if I had stayed simply as a typist using a manual typewriter in a little construction office, my first full time job after leaving college.

The same approach works now. When you do temporary work, you are often forced to adapt to and learn about new machines and new procedures. This educates you so that you have more skills to offer a prospective employer.

There are other ways of finding a new job. I suggest that you go to the library and read books that are available there on job hunting. They offer helpful suggestions about your personal appearance, how to handle an interview, how to write resumes, and ways of learning the kinds of jobs in which you be the happiest as well as the most skilled.

Getting a new job takes work, self discipline, and planning. It is not simply a question of walking into an employment agency, sitting down, and saying, "Well, here I am." You have got to do the work. The employment agency can help, but their help increases in direct proportion to how well you present yourself and how qualified you are.

Appearance and presentation count. I've had college graduates wander into my office, dressed in wrinkled cotton skirts, sweaters held together with safety pins, straggling long hair, unpolished shoes, hosiery with runs in them. I have never hired a person dressed this way, regardless of her other qualifications. My business involved day-to-day dealings with high level corporate clients. My feeling is that if you cannot take the time to clean up your personal appearance, if you choose to insult other people's values and sensibilities by dressing or behaving in a rude manner, you will be as lazy and slovenly in dealing with clients, and this kind of behavior will not make money for my company.

If you have just started a job which does not pay you benefits and which involves a long commute, stay there long enough to build a good working reputation so that you will get a good recommendation if you decide to leave. Even better, a good work history may allow you to get a significant raise or a promotion into an area of work that will pay you more and provide on-the-job training. If possible, attend night school to learn new skills so that you can move to a higher paying job.

After evaluating your job, look at your car. If you are making payments on a car, you should probably keep the car and keep up with the payments. When your car is paid for, however, drive it until it drops. Do not rush out to buy a new car. If you keep your old car, you will have to keep it in excellent repair and that means routine and frequent oil changes. Find a mechanic you can trust. As soon as you hear strange noises, take that car to your mechanic. Ask him to drive it around with you in it to be sure he hears what you hear. Ask him to tell you what he thinks is wrong, how much it will cost, what kind of guarantee he makes on his repairs.

As soon as your car loan is paid off, talk with your insurance agent about whether you should continue to carry collision and comprehensive insurance. The amount you pay for insurance may not be worthwhile in terms of the age and condition of your car.

After your job and your car, examine your "home economics." Take one or two products that you purchase and chose to make them yourself. Take one or two convenience foods-- salad dressings, lunch meats, packaged bread stuffings, TV dinners--and learn to make them yourself, from scratch. I am not suggesting that you give up every convenience food, but choose one or two, and routinely make them yourself. Whatever it is that you choose to cook from scratch, each week take the money you would have spent buying the ready-made product and put it into your savings account or a convenient cookie jar. I don't care if it's only $5 a week. Stash it away where you cannot spend it immediately. Let's assume that you save $5 a week for 52 weeks or $260 for the year cooking some foods from scratch rather than buying them ready made.

If you eat your lunches at a restaurant, decide to make your lunches at home for 3 days out of 5. Take the money you would have spent at the restaurant, and put it in your savings account or cookie jar. DO NOT SPEND IT ON ANYTHING ELSE. Similarly, if you give your children lunch money or money for after school snacks, make their lunches for one day a week and put the money you would have given them into your savings account. Let's assume that by making these lunches, you save $15 a week for 52 weeks, for a total of $780 for the year.

During the coming year, sew at least three items of clothing for yourself that you would ordinarily have bought. Maybe you plan to buy a new vest, a new casual jacket, a new skirt. You can sew a similar item for at least half of what you would pay for it in the store, and then take the money you saved to your savings account. Let's assume that you save $20 per item or $60 for the year.

Stop smoking. I believe that a package of cigarettes costs about $1.80 each now. If you eliminate 10 packs a week, for fifty-two weeks you save $936.

Eliminate professional nail care. Put the money you would have spent into the bank. If you spend $7 every 6 weeks on nail care, eliminating this service will save you about $56 a year.

Cut or trim your children's hair at least four times a year. Let's assume that you have two children, and it costs $7 each time you take them to the barber. Four x $7 = $28 x two children = $56 for the year.

You decide to cut down the number of long distance and toll telephone calls you make to save $5 a month, for 12 months = $60 a year.

You do not charge anything on your credit cards until you have brought the balances down to the place where you can pay them off each month, without paying any service charges. Let's assume you had $500 on your revolving charge card, on which you are paying about 18% interest, or about $90 a year. You eliminate these balances and save yourself $90. Actually, you will save more than this, because you are not paying interest on interest.

Assume that with the money you are saving by making your lunches and sewing, you manage to accumulate a balance of $700 in your savings account. You transfer this amount to your checking account, and you talk with your banker to make sure that by doing this you save the $7 a month service charge. Seven dollars x 12 months = $84.00. In order to keep from spending this money, I do not carry it as part of the balance in my checkbook. I know it's there, but it doesn't show up on my balance so I do not think about spending it. I just let it stay there, hidden from my sight, working for me by saving checking account charges.

Now, purchasing clothes. Assume that you do not buy that green dress you like so well because you know you would have to buy matching shoes and handbag. That saves you about $150. Budget the money saved and put it into your savings account.

Now, add up what you might have saved for the coming year by taking the actions described above: Do not include any job changes or any changes in your car payments, but only include **short term** consumption habits. Do not include the cigarette smoking either unless you have actually quit.

Do it yourself cooking	$260 per year
Make your own lunches	$780
Sew 3 items of clothing	$ 60
Eliminate professional nail care	$ 56
Cut your own or your children's hair	$ 56
Lower your phone bill	$ 60
Eliminate interest on your charge cards	$ 90
Eliminate checking account fees.	$ 84
Controlled clothing purchase	$150
Total Saved for the Year	**$1,596.00**

This is money that you have saved and that is not taxable by the Internal Revenue Service.

The important thing is to actually *save* the money you have saved. Don't spend it on other consumer items. The way to do this is to take the money you would have spent and deposit it directly into your savings account. Do not spend it on some other item of consumption.

One of my favorite tales about silly financial behavior comes from one of my friends, who has two small children. Her husband bought an expensive pair of athletic shoes for one of the children, and paid full price for the shoes even though they were supposed to have been on sale. My friend packed her two children into the car, drove to the mall to confront the sales clerk with the shoes. No problem there. My friend received a refund of $15 for overpayment on the shoes. By then, however, the kids were cranky and hungry, so my friend ended up spending the $15 on lunches at a fast food restaurant for the children and herself. She also spent money on gas and wear and tear on the car driving to and from the mall. Obviously, she did not save any money on this trip despite the refund on the athletic shoes.

In order to save money, to hang onto it after you have saved it, you need to lock it up some place where you can't get to it easily. One of the easiest places to put it away is U.S. Savings Bonds, which have been paying a minimum rate of 6% interest-- higher than any bank (at the time I am writing this book). Savings bonds are absolutely safe, and the interest on them is tax deferred until you cash them in. Since you don't receive any interest on them until you cash them in, you can't go out and spend the interest, so they force you to save. Another important feature of Savings Bonds is that you can buy one for as little as $25. Parents who buy Savings Bonds after December 31, 1989, and use the money to pay for college tuition, may pay no income tax on the interest they earn. You can buy Savings Bonds at your local bank without charge. Discuss the various bonds and the tax provisions with your banker.

Another way to lock up money you've saved is to invest it in a high quality common stock. If you buy a high quality stock, keep the stock certificates in your safe deposit box. You can use stock certificates as collateral to borrow against if you need a small short term loan.

Borrowing money to save money seems like a stupid idea, but I used to do it all the time because I was very good at making loan payments and very poor at making payments into my savings account. So, despite the loss incurred in interest charges, I used to borrow $2,000 to buy stock, and then pay off the loan as quickly as possible. Then I held onto the stock, and usually, the stock increased in price and my savings grew. Whenever I sold a stock, I *never* spent the money. I reinvested it into another stock or mutual fund. The point was that once I bought that stock, I could hold onto it. I would not simply spend it away.

If you buy a stock, ask that the dividends be automatically reinvested in more stock. Not all stocks do this, but mutual funds will automatically reinvest. That way, your dividends and interest earned will turn around and buy more stock to earn more dividends and interest, another way of locking up your money. This is called **compounding** -- you are earning money on your interest as well as on your principal. Compounding makes a big difference in how much money you can earn. For example, if you put $10,000 into an investment yielding 8% interest, and you leave all your interest or dividends to be reinvested, at the end of six years your original $10,000 will be worth $16, 160.

If you have all your dividends and capital gains reinvested monthly, keep very careful records for your income tax return. The IRS has made automatic reinvesting a record keeping nightmare, but it's worth the time in record keeping in terms of the money you earn on your reinvestments.

A third way of locking up money so you can't spend it is to prepay your mortgage. If you have a thirty year mortgage of $85,000 at 10% interest and you prepay only $25 each month, you save a total of 57 mortgage payments and you save $35,286 in interest.

Saving money is as much a psychological problem as a financial problem. You've got to figure out what works for you, but to obtain capital, you must first save. That's why buying a house is such a good way to save. You can't go spend your house easily, unless you make the mistake of getting a home equity loan.

People find it difficult to believe that little things count, but little things day after day add up, and pretty soon, you are talking about serious money. People don't like to bother with the little things. It seems undignified, petty, even silly, but you can see that little things add up, as shown above. If you save $100 a month ($25.00 per week) and invest the money in a mutual fund earning 8% interest per year, you will have $48,009 at the end of 18 years, about enough money to send one child through college depending on the school. You say, "I don't have $100 a month to invest," but in the example above, I showed that it is possible to save $1500 in one year by sewing, cooking, paying off your credit card debt. That comes to more than $100 a month.

Earning and saving money takes work, consistent self discipline, and patience. It also takes some thought. I have tried to teach you "thinking" tools throughout this book to help you accumulate money reorienting your life rather than just "comparison shopping" in the supermarkets. If you follow these precepts, you will be rewarded in the long run.

CHAPTER FOURTEEN: WHEN YOU HAVE MONEY, WHAT THEN?

The scope of this book does not include how to invest your money after you have accumulated it. However, there are a few things I'd like to mention that you should consider now, whether you have money or not.

First, you should have a will. This is the only way you can insure that your assets go where you want them in the event of your death. Joint ownership of assets is no guarantee that they will go where you want them to go. Without a will, the state in which you live will distribute your assets according to their laws and procedures, which means that the court will approve certain expenditures, will have its own accounting requirements, will have its own rules for dividing your assets between your spouse and your children.

Second, if you appoint guardians for your children in your will, you should also carry a life insurance policy that pays the proceeds to the guardian in case of your death. I had a friend who appointed her brother as guardian for her two children, but her brother was an impoverished artist with barely enough money to care for his own children. My friend did not think to buy life insurance, making her brother the beneficiary so he would have the money to care for her children.

Third you should give a power of attorney to a trusted relative or friend in case you become disabled. If you become disabled, someone will have to make the decisions regarding your care, the care of your children, how to pay for this care.

Fourth, I believe you should have a living will and a medical power of attorney. A living will outlines what level of care you wish to have if you are disabled and to what extent hospitals and doctors should intervene to keep you alive. The medical power of attorney allows someone you trust to make these decisions for you if you are unable to do so.

After you accumulate about $2,000, you will want to invest this money in such a way that it will begin to produce money for you while you sleep. If you work at a job that does not pay you any type of pension, plan to invest your money in an Individual Retirement Account. I believe you should have a "self directed" IRA; that is, one where you make decisions about how your money will be invested. You will need some financial institution to act as your trustee for your IRA. If it is a self-directed IRA, this will most likely be some sort of brokerage firm, preferably a discount broker. Shop around though for a firm that charges you the lowest rates for handling your IRA. Discuss with each firm what kinds of investments they recommend. Banks put you into their own certificates of deposit, and at present rates, I do not recommend them.

If you have no other pension, except an IRA you can deduct the $2,000 you invest each year from your income taxes, and the interest earned on your investment is tax deferred until you withdraw it upon your retirement. The tax rules governingR IA's are complex, but every bank and nearly every other financial institution provides information on IRA's. They are all eager to have your IRA money, so choose with care where you decide to place it.

Investing opens up an entirely new world of financial management. This world is exciting but complex, and you should begin to read, read, read now so you are prepared to enter this world. I suggest that you read such publications as *Money* and *The Kiplinger Letter* for information on changes in tax law, the performance of various mutual funds and stocks, how to pick and deal with various consultants such as tax accountants, lawyers, and financial planners.

I also recommend that you read overall personal money management books, such as *Making the Most of Your Money* by Jane Bryant Quinn. Sylvia Porter is another well known financial advisor who offers excellent advice on money management for average people. Most magazines now offer advice as do many newspapers. You should read these articles daily. Cut them out and save them for future reference.

At first, it may be difficult for you to understand what is being said. The language will be new. I've tried to give you an introduction to some of the language throughout this book. But don't worry. Keep a good dictionary at hand and with time, you will also learn to decipher the meaning of specific words through the context in which they appear in the articles.

You will need to read for the rest of your life, because our society is so dynamic, so constantly changing, that financial rules go out the window almost every year. In my lifetime, the income tax laws have changed profoundly under the influence of equal rights for women. The rules affecting capital gains appear to be a football that congress plays with during every election year. The rules affecting individual retirement accounts were changed just a few years ago, but congress is under pressure to change them again.

When you accumulate money, you acquire the Internal Revenue Service looking over your shoulder more carefully. This means, you've got to keep your records absolutely faithfully and in good order. The magazines named above offer advice on how to handle an IRS audit if you are subjected to one. They keep you informed of tax law changes. They tell you what records to keep and how to keep them.

Remember, the only way to learn is through doing it: investing your money. If you read and use some judgment and caution, you should make money for yourself. You will lose some, but on balance, you will come out ahead if you are not a sucker for a "fast buck." I have lost money, quite a bit of money in fact. I have let my feelings overrule my head. I have trusted investment advisors who should not have been trusted. I did not know enough about investing at the time to be able to judge their performance and qualifications. Remember, if it sounds too good to be true, it probably is too good to be true.

Nonetheless, when I have bought quality stocks and mutual funds as listed and recommended in various financial magazines and newspaper columns, I have made money. When I have bought houses that I loved in neighborhoods that offered many amenities, I have made money. When I have consistently refused to be enticed into the "American Dream" of more, more, more, I have made money. When you keep your **net worth** statement year after year, you can monitor your progress.

I know, because I've done it. You can do it too. Remember, if you want to retire comfortably, in today's dollars you will need between $250,000 and $300,000 in **capital** to provide you with a **pretax** income of between $20,000 - $30,000 a year. How far along are you toward this goal? Check your net worth statements. They will tell you.

GLOSSARY OF TERMS

After tax dollars -- wages and other income remaining after taxes and social security have been subtracted or withheld.

Amortization-- to liquidate a debt over a period of payments, or to spread the costs of tool or piece of equipment over a period of time or a series of uses.

Appreciation -- the opposite of depreciation; an increase in value over time.

Arbitraging -- playing interest rate spreads to earn money; buying securities in one market to sell them in another market to take advantage of price differences.

Assets -- those things that a person owns that comprise his wealth, or capital; those things that can be used to improve one's life in a physical, mental, or social sense; things or qualities that are considered valuable.

Capital, capital goods, capital assets -- money and equipment that earn money for you; any form of wealth used to accumulate more wealth.

Capital gain -- in federal tax law, money earned on capital, usually in the form of stocks and bonds; **capital gains** presently taxed at a 28% rate.

Capital investment -- money invested in tools or equipment or securities or other forms of wealth that earn money for the investor.

Comparison shop -- to compare the prices of similar or the same goods and services offered by different stores, banks, companies, etc. The object of comparison shopping is usually to pay the lowest price for the goods or services.

Compounding, compound interest -- interest payments made upon principal and accrued interest.

Deficit -- a shortage, the amount by which a given sum of money falls short from what was expected.

Depreciation -- decline in value over time.

Disposable income -- money left over after all necessities, such as food and shelter, have been paid for, money available for non-essential goods and services.

Economies of scale -- buying in large quantities at lower prices to spread the costs of any goods or services over a larger number of people.

Equity -- the value of any property after all the debts against it have been paid.

Fixed expenses, fixed costs -- usually recurring expenses over which a person has little control; costs that do not vary from month to month; costs that cannot easily be changed, such as mortgage payments or car payments.

Fringe benefits -- benefits such as vacation time, medical insurance, health insurance provided by companies to their employees either free of direct charge to the employee or only partially paid for by the employee.

Gross income --income before any deductions for taxes or insurance or social security have been withheld.

Hidden costs -- any costs associated with goods or services that are not specifically included in the base or sticker price.

Image -- a concept or facade perceived by the public; a picture or presentation of self that may not represent the true self or the inner self.

Inflation -- the rise in prices caused by too much money in the economy in relation to the amount of goods available for purchase; the gradual decrease in the purchasing power of the dollar.

Interest -- money paid for the use of money. Banks pay interest for the use of savers' money; banks and companies charge interest to consumers who use their money through charge cards or loans.

Leverage -- the amount of debt relative to one's equity.

Liabilities -- the opposite of assets; obligations or debts; impairments.

Long term -- a time span of more than six months.

Median income -- that point where half the U.S. population earns less and half earns more; in 1991 median family income was $34,788.

Networking -- using a group of friends, relations, business associates to help one locate a new job; using such people to gain access to jobs, organizations, sources of capital, etc.

Net worth -- the wealth remaining after all debts or liabilities have been paid.

Non taxable, tax free, tax exempt -- income that is not subject to most taxes and/or social security withholding.

Pantry -- a place to store food, a stock of food.

Pretax -- wages and other income before taxes and social security have been withheld; gross income.

Principal -- the capital or wealth upon which interest can be charged; the main body of money.

Rate of return -- the percentage interest rate paid for the use of money.

Short term -- in financial markets, a time span of six months of less.

Status -- social standing, high social standing or prestige.

Tax deferred -- income on which federal taxes are not paid until the income is actually withdrawn from the investment for personal use; Individual Retirement Accounts are one example.

Tax exempt -- income on which no federal taxes are paid.

Tax sheltered -- money invested into assets that is protected from federal and local taxes until the asset is sold.

Time versus money -- the concept of translating hours worked into dollars earned; calculating the trade-off between one's available time and one's available money.

INDEX

Index

A

B

C

D

E

F

J

K

L

Q

R

S

T

NOTES